NUCLEAR ETHICS

NUCLEAR ETHICS

A Christian Moral Argument

DAVID HOLLENBACH, S.J.

PAULIST PRESS New York/Ramsey

Acknowledgments

An earlier version of this essay was presented at the Fifth Annual Colloquium of Catholic Bishops and Scholars, in Washington, D.C., September,
1982. The colloquium is jointly sponsored by the Joint Committee of Catholic
Learned Societies and Scholars and the National Conference of Catholic
Bishops' Committee on Doctrine. I am grateful to those who organized and
participated in the colloquium for providing me with the opportunity to
develop these thoughts in an atmosphere of mutually constructive criticism.
The essay presented at the colloquium was published as "Nuclear Weapons
and Nuclear War: The Shape of the Catholic Debate," in *Theological Studies*
43 (December, 1982). Walter J. Burghardt, the editor of *Theological Studies*,
has graciously permitted me to publish this more developed form of the
earlier essay. Comparison of the two versions will reveal some shifts in my own
thinking in a relatively short period of time. Such developments can be
expected and hoped for in the continuing public debate. Finally, I want to
thank Joan Nuth for her superb assistance in preparing the manuscript for
publication.

Library of Congress
Catalog Card Number: 83-80365

ISBN: 0-8091-2546-3

Published by Paulist Press
545 Island Road, Ramsey, N.J. 07446

Printed and bound in the
United States of America

Contents

For my friends
Margaret Farley
and
John Langan

Introduction

Argument about nuclear policy has been a fact of public life in the West since the awesome power at the heart of matter was first unleashed during the Second World War. This ongoing debate has assumed a number of distinct forms through these years, forms which have been influenced by the political climate prevailing between the superpowers, by the state of the relations between members of the Atlantic Alliance, by the development of new technological capacities, by the proliferation of nuclear weapons, and by the level of public awareness and understanding of nuclear policy questions.[1]

Recent events clearly show that the state of the nuclear question is assuming a new form in the present moment. U.S./U.S.S.R. relations are at a most delicate and dangerous point. Tensions have increased significantly in the aftermath of Soviet actions in Afghanistan and Poland. These tensions are reflected in the U.S. Senate's nonratification of the SALT II treaty and in the acrimonious exchanges at the Helsinki Accord review conference in Madrid. At the same time, however, the two sets of negotiations underway in Geneva on strategic arms reductions and on the control of intermediate range nuclear forces in Europe have opened at least a slim possibility of new developments in arms control. The new state of the question is also shaped by the significant strains which have recently developed within NATO.[2] A significant intellectual debate has begun within the Alliance about the wisdom of a

1

NATO declaratory policy renouncing the first use of nuclear weapons.[3] Further, technological developments have created the possibility of deploying formidable new first-strike weapons, such as MX and Trident II, and weapons which are difficult to detect both before and after they are launched, such as the cruise missile. Possession and deployment of such new weapons by both superpowers will raise the level of uncertainty and danger in the balance of terror by a significant degree. Finally, all these changes have converged to bring the fear of nuclear war and the issues of nuclear policy to the center of public concern on both sides of the Atlantic.[4] This fear has sparked the European peace movement, the campaign for a nuclear arms freeze in the United States, the activities of groups such as Physicians for Social Responsibility, and the outpouring of public sentiment at the large demonstration in New York during the UN Special Session on Disarmament in June, 1982.

These developments have set the context for a serious new engagement by the churches in this debate. In particular, the Roman Catholic Church in the United States has embarked on a course that has thrust it into public argument on a central matter of government policy in a way that is almost certainly unique in its history. The uniqueness of this level of Church involvement makes it imperative that Church leaders—bishops, clergy, religious and laity alike—become as clear as possible about the relation between the central realities of the Christian faith and the host of complex issues which swirl through the clouds of public discussion.

This effort at a deep moral and religious reappraisal of Christian responsibilities in the area of nuclear policy has caused a variety of frequently conflicting conclusions to emerge within the churches. This essay will present a sketch of some of the major positions which have emerged. It will also attempt to identify the reasons—theological, political and military—which account for the divergences among these positions. It will offer an assessment of these positions and propose a basic theological approach to the moral issues in nuclear policy for consideration and further debate. The focus of this exploration will be on developments within the Catholic community, although these developments will be set against the horizon of the larger theological and secular debate.

The structure of the analysis will be the following. In Part One the broad theological perspectives which shape Christian moral analysis of the nuclear question will be outlined. This part will examine the tensions between the pacifist and just war traditions which have come visibly to the surface in contemporary Christian debate. Chapter 1 looks at these tensions historically, Chapter 2 from a more analytical philosophical and political perspective, and Chapter 3 from an explicitly theological vantage point. The general argument of Part One is that the pacifist and just war approaches to the morality of warfare are complementary and that both are needed as the Christian community approaches the nuclear debate. Part Two gets more specific and addresses the actual issues which dominate current policy discussions. This part moves from broad perspectives to more detailed moral argument. Chapter 4 reviews the traditional just war criteria and shows their relevance to nuclear policy. Chapter 5 deals specifically with the morality of any possible use of nuclear weapons. Chapter 6 seeks a morally and politically reasonable way to deal with the perplexing and paradoxical question of nuclear deterrence. The Conclusion sums up the major proposals of the essay.

One very important element of the current debate within the Church will be notable by its absence from the discussion in these pages. The single most important contribution by the churches to the contemporary discussion of United States nuclear policy has been that of the National Conference of Catholic Bishops Ad Hoc Committee on War and Peace. The final version of the Committee's pastoral letter on this subject is expected to be voted on and issued sometime in 1983. In order to avoid entering into arguments which could easily be irrelevant when the final version of the letter is approved, it seemed best to put forward my views on their own merits.

So this essay should be regarded as the effort of one theologian to contribute to the debate which will surely continue well beyond the time when the final pastoral letter is issued. The moral argument on nuclear policy is unlikely to be resolved in a short time. This essay will have achieved its purpose if it makes some contribution to the further formation of intelligent theological and moral argument in the Church on this most urgent question of our time.

Part One

Perspectives:
Pacifism and
Just War Theory

Chapter 1

Historical Traditions in Tension

Over the past thirty years a significant reevaluation of the basic Christian posture toward the morality of warfare has been underway within the Roman Catholic Church. It is well known that the just war theory has occupied the central place in the Catholic tradition's response to moral questions concerning the use of force. Several recent studies have pointed out that as recently as the late 1950s the just war theory was the only officially sanctioned Catholic approach to the morality of warfare.[1] For example, in 1956 Pope Pius XII denied that Roman Catholic citizens could be conscientious objectors to military service in conflicts conducted within the bounds of the just war norms.[2] The pope's negative words on conscientious objection were spoken in the context of teachings which denied the moral legitimacy of modern total warfare and which urgently called for the development of structures of international organization adequate to the task of peacemaking. Nevertheless, his rejection of conscientious objection amounted to a rejection of pacifism as an authentic moral option for the Catholic citizen.

Since the papacy of John XXIII and the Second Vatican Council, this clear rejection of the pacifist stance has been undergoing reevaluation and modification. From his study of the relevant papal, conciliar and episcopal documents, J. Bryan Hehir has shown that during recent decades "the principal development has been the legitimation of a pacifist perspec-

tive as a method for evaluating modern warfare."[3] Official
approbation of conscientious objection as a legitimate Catholic
stance and serious questioning of the justification of any warfare in the nuclear age are important new themes in Catholic
teaching on warfare since Vatican II. This shift in official
teaching has been partly the cause and partly the result of the
emergence of a visible and articulate pacifist movement within the Catholic community. Though the Catholic Church has
not become a totally pacifist church, it can no longer be said
that just war theory is *the* Catholic approach to the morality of
warfare.

Thus the moral argument within the Church about nuclear weapons policies is being shaped in part by a more fundamental debate about the relation between pacifism, just war
theory, and the central religious convictions of the Christian
faith. Because just war theory is no longer an ethical posture
which can be taken for granted in Catholic discussion, questions of a more basic theological nature have come to the fore
in the nuclear debate. The reality of pluralism on the level of
ethics is compelling the Church to a consideration of the
relation between faith in Jesus Christ and the problems of war
and violence. In other words, the new state of the question
calls for the development of a properly *theological* approach to
the ethics of war and peace in the nuclear age.

In order to understand this development, it is worth noting that the complete renunciation of the use of violence has
been present in one strand of Catholic tradition from the time
of Jesus down to the present day. Studies of the early Christian
attitudes toward military service have found no evidence that
Christians served in the military up until approximately the
year 170 or 180 A.D.[4] Also, during these earliest years there is
no evidence that the patristic authors presented theological
justification for such participation. After 170, Christians began
to move into the army in increasing numbers. At the time of
Constantine, when the status of Christianity shifted from that
of a persecuted minority to that of the official religion of the
Roman empire, Christians became responsible for the governance and administration of society. As a result of this changed

place in society, Christian participation in the military became much more general. This social development was accompanied by the elaboration of moral theological norms setting limits to legitimate warfare and to Christian participation in warfare. These norms have gradually been refined into what has come to be known as the just war theory or the just war tradition.

The history of this development during the patristic period, however, is more complex than it is sometimes understood to have been. To portray the development as a process in which an early pacifism was gradually but thoroughly replaced by the just war ethic would be to distort what actually occurred. On the one hand, the non-participation of the earliest Christians was a consequence of their religious objections to killing and violence. But it was also the result of the fact that most of the earliest Christians were not Roman citizens and were thus ineligible to serve in the Roman forces. In addition, the ordinary level of sexual morality of Roman soldiers (who were officially forbidden to marry), the encouragement of emperor worship among the armed forces, and other practices of Roman civil religion common among soldiers were additional reasons for the non-participation of Christians. The three capital sins against which the patristic writers took their strongest stands were homicide, adultery and idolatry. Early Christian objection to military service appears to be based on the desire to avoid all three of these dangers, and not simply on an objection to killing or on a fully developed ethic of nonviolence.[5]

At the same time that Christians were beginning to serve in the military forces in larger numbers, however, these same reasons for non-participation continued to be pressed by some members of the Church. The pacifist stance was not totally replaced. Rather it continued to be present as *one* of the Christian moral postures toward warfare. Writers such as Tertullian and Lactantius took what had been a less than fully articulated Christian objection to the killing involved in warfare and made it into the central theme of their theological evaluations of military activity. It appears that the same changes in the place of the Church in society which led to the development of the just war theory were also the occasion for the emergence of a more self-conscious and coherent ethic of nonviolence within the Church. Considerations such as these indicate that the popular view that the Constantinian revolution transformed the Christian ethic from a pacifist commitment to nonviolence to a just war willingness to legitimate some forms of the use of force is oversimplified. As Knut Ruyter has observed, "On the basis of the sources, the picture seems to be more complex and pluriform."[6]

This pluriformity in the Christian response to warfare was given institutional expression as the distinction between the lay and monastic forms of life developed within the Church. The earliest Christians' refusal to take up arms became the particular evangelical witness and vocation of monks, while the laity held responsibility for the governance of secular society.[7] The history of medieval Christian political thought shows that this "lay" ethic was based on both natural political reason and on an effort to embody the gospel in the institutions of social life. Nevertheless, the rapid growth of monastic life in the post-Constantinian period was in part the result of the conviction among numbers of Christians that the teachings of the gospel were being compromised by the growing engagement of the Church in the affairs of "the world."[8] The monastic response to this situation was withdrawal from participation in the prevailing institutions of economic, familial and political life and positive commitment to the evangelical counsels of poverty, chastity and obedience lived in community. The nonparticipation of monks in military activity was one aspect of this effort to embody the teaching and example of Jesus in a concrete sociological form. As Roland Bainton has put it, "The prime transmitters of the nonmilitary tradition of the early church were the monks."[9] This pacifist ethic has also been handed on in ecumenical Christianity by Protestant communities such as the Mennonites, the Swiss Brethren and the Quakers. Thus contemporary pacifist Christians who have become major participants in the debate within the Catholic Church on the nuclear question are heirs to a tradition which has been alive throughout the history of the Church. This tradition has been in tension with just war thinking. Most often it has been largely overshadowed by the more dominant ethic of the limited legitimacy of the use of force. Aberrant phenomena such as the crusades, the creation of military religious orders like the Knights Templar, and the raising of papal armies almost extinguished the non-military tradition at some points in the history of the Church. But it would be inaccurate to say that the non-military tradition was abandoned in the centuries following Constantine and Augustine.[10] If we are to understand the historical roots of the contemporary debate between pacifist and just war thinkers this long-standing pluralism must be fully taken into account.

The tension present in the history of the Christian response to warfare continues in the contemporary theological argument. Just as the early monks regarded the increasing engagement of Christians and the Church in the affairs of the world as a betrayal of the teachings and example of Jesus Christ, so today there are those in the Christian community who regard Christian reliance on just war thinking as unfaithfulness to the gospel. For example, James W. Douglass has stated this position straightforwardly:

> Inasmuch as war's central action of *inflicting* suffering and death is directly opposed to the example of Christ in *enduring* these same realities, the Church has reason for repentance in having allowed herself to become involved since the age of Constantine in an ethic which would justify what conflicts with the essence of the Gospel.[11]

This statement must be taken with the greatest seriousness in the current debate on peace, war and nuclear arms, for it makes a claim about the essence of the gospel. It was this claim which led the early monks to adopt a form of life which differed from the posture of the established Church of post-Constantinian Christendom. It is the same claim which underlies one of Thomas Aquinas's arguments for the non-participation of clerics in military activity:

> All the clerical orders are directed to the ministry of the altar, on which the Passion of Christ is represented sacramentally, according to 1 Cor xi.26: "As often as you shall eat this bread, and drink this chalice, you shall show the death of the Lord, until He come." Wherefore it is unbecoming for them to slay or shed blood, and it is more fitting that they should be ready to shed their own blood for Christ, so as to imitate in deed what they portray in their ministry.[12]

Though neither the early monks nor Thomas Aquinas rejected the participation of all Christians in warfare, it is important that they did see an intrinsic connection between nonviolence, the Passion of Christ, and the Church's ministry of word and sacrament. The vocation of monks and clerics was to bear witness to this connection through a distinctive, more evangelical form of life.[13]

This Thomistic way of responding to the historical tension between just war and pacifist traditions has lost much of its social plausibility and theological foundation today. The differentiation of roles, gradation of status, and organic, hierarchical structure of medieval society provided the social context within which St. Thomas could speak of a clearly defined difference between the responses to warfare appropriate for the layperson or cleric. From a sociological point of view, the medieval differentiation of ethical responsibilities according to a stable structure of established roles has been replaced by a modern conviction that responsibility is based on "the self as such, [on] the individual regardless of his position in society."[14] From a theological point of view, following the Second Vatican Council the Church has strongly affirmed that the fullness of holiness is the vocation of every Christian (layperson, religious and cleric alike).[15] Restriction of the full evangelical challenge to a group of religious specialists is theologically illegitimate in light of this development. There has also been an important theological recovery of the fact that the Church's mission and witness in the world are rooted in the baptism which is common to all Christians and in the eucharist in which all Christians share.

In light of these social and theological developments, therefore, the pacifist challenge to the just war tradition has become central for the Church as a whole and for all its members. One must ask (to paraphrase St. Thomas): if there is indeed a fundamental congruence between the Passion of Christ and the renunciation of violent force, should not the Church as a whole "imitate in deed" what it portrays in the baptismal and eucharistic life in which all Christians participate?

We will seriously misunderstand the theological basis of the just war theory if we do not accept the full weight of this question. There can be no doubt that the New Testament proclaims a message of peace and calls those who would be Jesus' disciples to a nonviolent way of living. This proclamation and call are evident in Jesus' teachings on love of neighbor and love of enemy.[16] They are embodied in Jesus' renunciation of violent revolutionary tactics of resistance to the oppressive Roman occupation of Palestine.[17] Most centrally, the death of Jesus on the cross was an unjust execution of an innocent man. Though the full meaning of the crucifixion cannot be reduced to its ethical significance, it is impossible for Christian theology to avoid the challenge of nonviolence that the crucifix presents. John Howard Yoder has argued that the redemptive and saving significance of the cross is inseparable from its nonviolent witness to the value which the love of God has given to every human life. In Yoder's view the moral call to an ethic of nonviolence and the redemptive action of God in Christ are unified in the crucifixion.

> The prohibition of killing is expanded by its juxtaposition with the work of the cross. As Cain's fratricide is prototypical of the rebellion of the race (I John 3:11f, 15) so Christ's sacrifice for others is a model of our community love

> (3:16). . . . As at the beginning in the covenants with Cain
> and Noah, life was the supreme good needing protection,
> the shedding of blood being the only necessary prohibition;
> so in light of the cross, the bodily life of the neighbor, even
> of the enemy, is revealed as the prerequisite and the proto-
> type of all other values needing protection, even died for, in
> and for the neighbor, even the enemy.[18]

And, as Stanley Hauerwas has put it, the cross of Jesus reveals
to us "the kind of suffering that is to be expected when the
power of non-resistant love challenges the powers that rule
this world by violence."[19]

An ethical analysis of war and peace that seeks its roots in
the central religious identity of Christianity must acknowledge, therefore, that the values of human life, peace and
nonviolence make urgent demands upon the Christian conscience. That the just war tradition, *when it is rightly interpreted,* begins from such an acknowledgment is evident from a
consideration of what James Turner Johnson has called "the
original just war question." On the basis of his extensive studies
of the history of just war thinking, Johnson has shown that this
question "arises again and again in patristic and medieval
writers concerned with Christian participation in violence. Put
generally, it is the query, 'May a Christian ever morally take
part in violence?' "[20] The treatment of warfare in Thomas
Aquinas's classic discussion of the topic put the question even
more strongly than does Johnson. The *quaestio* with which
Thomas begins his reflection is this: "Is it *always* a sin to fight
in war?"[21] The just war tradition, therefore, is not the result of
ignorance or rejection of the biblical and theological evidence
of Jesus Christ's challenge to a peaceful and nonviolent way of
life. Rather the just war tradition, again when it is properly
understood, rests on the conviction that violent warfare should
be presumed to be morally unacceptable and even sinful.

It is both theologically inaccurate and culturally disastrous
if this presupposition is forgotten. In Johnson's view such a loss
of historical memory is exactly what has happened in recent
centuries in discussions of the just war tradition.

It is one of the sad ironies of history that this origin of the just war tradition has been so badly remembered as to turn it inside out: rather than a sign of a reluctance to justify violence for Christians, the tradition has come to be regarded, and not only by pacifists, as an attempt to declare the need to justify Christian resort to violence a non-question, a question that has already been answered. . . . An attempt to

recollect again, in and for the Christian community, what this original just war question was about leads to the somewhat startling discovery that pacifist and non-pacifist just war Christians have something profoundly in common: a searching distrust of violence.[22]

Gordon Zahn goes even further than does Johnson in his negative reading of the history. He has pointed out that, as the theory evolved historically, the presumption against the use of violence was replaced by a presumption of the justice of warfare conducted by legitimate authority. In Zahn's view, this reversal "reduces the whole elaborate formulation of the just war and its carefully developed conditions to little more than a meaningless copybook exercise."[23] Though Zahn underestimates the importance of the necessary role of government in reaching decisions about the morality of the resort to arms, he is surely correct about the devastating effects of this shift of presuppositions. Under *no* circumstances can war be considered a good. And for Christians, it is impossible to *presume* that the resort to lethal force is compatible with respect for the sacredness of human life or fidelity to the gospel of Christ. The original just war question implies that nonviolence is the Christian norm and that the use of force can only be moral by way of exception, if at all. Violent force should be *presumed* to be incompatible with a fundamental Christian moral orientation.

Chapter 2

The Relation
of Justice and Peace

This historical sketch shows that the contemporary argument between pacifism and just war theory must not be viewed as a disagreement between persons who are opposed to war and those who are in favor of it. Both moral postures regard war as evil. Nevertheless the two traditions do have differing understandings of the nature of the Christian moral obligation to avoid this evil. For the pacifist this obligation is absolute. For the just war thinker it is a conditional obligation which can be overridden in certain circumstances. The two approaches diverge in their evaluations of how to respond when the values of peace and nonviolence conflict with other important values such as the defense of the lives of innocent persons, the preservation of basic freedoms and human rights in the face of aggression, or the liberation of persons from situations of degrading poverty and political repression. From the point of view of the biblical witness as well as from the historical and contemporary experience of human beings it is evident that there are a number of different values which call out for human respect. Respect for human life and the preservation of peace make genuine claims on the Christian conscience. But so do the values of justice and human freedom. The dispute between pacifism and just war theory is rooted in their different understandings of how Christians should respond when these different values tragically conflict and are not simultaneously realizable in a concrete historical situation.

James Childress has made this point in the language of recent moral philosophy.[1] In Childress's reading, the just war theory rests on the conviction that we have a *prima facie* obligation not to harm or kill other human beings. A *prima facie* obligation is a genuine moral claim upon conscience, but it is conditional rather than absolute in nature. The condition which determines whether the *prima facie* duty of non-injury is our *actual* duty is that it must not conflict with another *prima facie* duty which is equally or more stringently binding in the concrete circumstances.[2]

For example, we have an obligation to keep the promises we have made. If, however, one is compelled to decide between keeping a promise to meet a friend for dinner and stopping on the roadside to aid a person injured in an automobile accident, the more stringent of these obligations should take precedence. This is not to say that promises should be broken whenever doing so would be of benefit to some third party. Promises should ordinarily be kept even at the cost of some genuine benefit to oneself or others.[3] As the parable of the good Samaritan indicates, however, relieving the suffering of a seriously injured victim can override even the obligations of priests and Levites in certain circumstances.

The logic of the just war theory has a similar structure. It does not maintain that killing is morally neutral and is justified whenever the deaths of certain people would be to the benefit of others or of society as a whole. Such a strictly utilitarian approach would deny the moral presumption against all killing that has been emphasized above. Thomas Aquinas comes uncharacteristically close to such a utilitarian justification for homicide when he defends capital punishment on the grounds that the individual person is related to the community "as part to whole" and may therefore be killed "that the common good may be preserved."[4] Germain Grisez has rightly objected that this line of reasoning could justify killing anyone whose death would bring benefit to the community as a whole.[5] As Grisez points out, such an argument has totalitarian implications and undercuts the notion that human beings have rights against society.

The question, then, is whether there are any obligations which are more stringent than the obligation not to use deadly force against human beings. Recent philosophical literature has debated this issue extensively. For example, Grisez has argued that the use of lethal force is morally permissible in repelling an unjust attack only when the intention is the protection of human life.[6] Life can be taken only in an action whose intent is the protection of life. Alan Donagan goes further and argues that the defensive use of force in such a conflict situation is obligatory. It is

> not merely permissible but a duty to employ force against
> the violent if their victims cannot otherwise be protected.
> Allowing for the impracticability of nice calculation, only
> necessary force is sanctioned. But if it is reasonably believed
> necessary to kill the attacker in order to save the victim, the
> attacker not only may be killed but ought to be.[7]

Donagan cites Leviticus 19:16 in support of his conclusion: "Neither shalt thou stand idly by the blood of thy neighbor."

Grisez and Donagan both believe, therefore, that the use of violence in the defense of human life is sometimes justified. The problem becomes more complex when the question concerns the use of force to protect goods other than human life, for example human freedom, national identity, or a just social order based on respect for the full range of human rights. Philosophers such as John Finnis have argued that the basic forms of human good are all equally fundamental. "There is no objective hierarchy amongst them."[8] The specific goods which Finnis regards as basic or fundamental are not relevant in this context. But his insistence that these goods are equally important aspects of human dignity has important implications for the way the just war theory is understood.[9] Can life be taken only in the defense of life, or is it justified in the defense of other goods such as freedom? To say that self-defense can justify the use of force does not tell us what is to count as self-defense. Is it defense of life, or of freedom, or of national identity, or what?

In a way that echoes Finnis, Paul Ramsey has recently argued that the basic human goods are incommensurable. They cannot be weighed against each other on the same scale. Thus Ramsey is hard pressed to find a way to evaluate a conflict situation where life must be taken if freedom is to be defended, or freedom sacrificed if life is held inviolable. If life and freedom are equally basic goods, how is one to choose between them when they conflict? Ramsey acknowledges that the outcome of the incommensurability of basic goods is a certain indeterminateness or ambiguity of moral judgment. He illustrates this conclusion in the following historical allusion to World War II:

> How can we decide whether the defense of Mother Russia against invasion and Hitler's plans to subjugate her people was worth the sacrifice of 20,000,000 Russian lives [Ramsey should add to this figure the millions of Germans killed also, I believe]. That, I say, is an indeterminate decision. There cannot be a knock-down argument either way. It is reasonable to say Russia should have defended herself at that toll. It is also reasonable to say the cost was too great. Those who say all modern war is disproportionate make the latter sort of judgment. Either verdict rests upon a comparison of lives lost with the value of nationhood having a continuous history. This entails a comparison of innumerable similarities and innumerable differences and interconnections between the clashing values; a comparison of very different types of good things. The upshot is indeterminacy in moral choice, either way.[10]

This example presents a challenge both to those who think some uses of violence can be justified and to those who reject such justification in all cases. In practice both groups grant priority to one fundamental human value or *prima facie* duty over another such value or duty. This is true of those who conclude that defense of freedom through the use of force can in some circumstances take priority over the prohibition against killing. It is equally true that those who reach the pacifist conclusion must be prepared to subordinate the obligation to protect the freedom of others to the obligation to protect human life. In a situation such as that described by Ramsey there is no evident solution which can insure the protection of all the values involved.

Finnis, Grisez and Ramsey have argued that the way out of this bind is through recognizing that our prime obligation is never to act *against* any of these fundamental values, even where inaction will lead to the loss of another such value. This solution, attractive though it may be from a theoretical point of view, does not do justice to the full range of our sense of moral obligation. Human beings do not only experience value as something never to be violated. We also experience value as something to be pursued actively. This is what it means to say we have a *prima facie* obligation to protect both human life and human freedom. In a situation like Ramsey's example of Russia in World War II, *some* decision must be made about whether life or freedom and national identity is to be given preference in action.

In an interchange with Ramsey, Richard McCormick has argued that even though human goods such as life and freedom are equally basic to human dignity, we must find some way to decide about the moral course of action in situations where these goods conflict. We are compelled to do so by the human condition itself. Responding to Ramsey's argument that the incommensurability of values can lead to two equally justifiable conclusions, McCormick states:

> If both conclusions are equally reasonable, we have not simply indeterminacy, but decisional paralysis. . . . What do we do? *Somehow or other,* in fear and trembling, we commensurate. In a sense we *adopt* a hierarchy.[11]

McCormick's language here has a voluntaristic ring to it. It suggests that we simply *choose* to make one or the other value more basic. Were this the case, then the question of whether it is pacifism or one or another form of just war theory that one espouses could only be answered on the basis of personal preference or the flip of a coin. Such a conclusion would place the entire edifice of social-political-military ethics on a foundation of sand, or on no foundation at all.

Despite the sound of this statement, McCormick certainly does not intend such an outcome. He believes that the human goods such as peace and justice or life and freedom are in some way "associated" with each other. They are not entirely independent variables. They are woven together in a more or less loosely knit fabric. In McCormick's view "the incommensurability of goods . . . is reduced by seeing them in interrelationship. And it is this interrelationship that provides the context—a kind of single scale—in which decisions are possible and reasonable, and that makes possible adoption of personal and community policies."[12] Here McCormick is not saying that goods such as peace and justice or life and freedom cannot conflict. Rather he is suggesting that there are certain characteristic ways in which the protection of life and the protection of freedom may be connected with each other. For example, regimes that regularly violate the right to freedom of conscience or of association are more than a little prone to employ techniques of torture and summary execution when this suits their political aims. Similarly, communities which hold life cheap are rarely known for their respect for other human rights and freedoms. This, I take it, is what McCormick is suggesting when he speaks of the interrelatedness of incommensurable goods.

Judgments such as these about the interdependence of basic goods evidently must be based on the historical experience of the human community. They cannot be arrived at *a priori* by meditating on the question of whether life or freedom or some other value is a greater good. The conclusions one reaches about these interrelations will be largely the result of generalizations about how human beings ordinarily can be expected to behave in their interactions with each other. In other words, they are prudential conclusions drawn from the lessons of history and from insight into "the way the world works." They are not purely moral or purely religious judgments. They involve both insight into basic human values plus a significant amount of worldly political wisdom.

It is on this level of practical political wisdom that one of the major points of dispute between the ethics of nonviolence and the just war theory is located. Just war thinking more explicitly employs conclusions of political reason in formulating its norms for military policy than does the tradition of nonviolence. Just war thinking sees the values of peace and justice as interrelated in a way that is not symmetrical. The protection of justice (that is, the securing of freedom and other fundamental human rights in a just social order) is regarded as a *prerequisite* for the establishment of a true and lasting peace. There is a causal linkage between the values which implies that a commitment to peace which does not rest on a prior commitment to justice will produce neither peace nor justice. As Pope John Paul II put it in his 1982 World Day of Peace Message:

> Peace can develop only where the elementary requirements of justice are safeguarded. . . . This is why Christians, even as they strive to resist and prevent every form of warfare, have no hesitation in recalling that, in the name of the elementary requirement of justice, peoples have a right and even a duty to protect their existence and freedom by proportionate means against an unjust aggressor.[13]

Of course this line of reasoning does not mean that the use of violent force is a legitimate way to redress all injustice. The "original just war question" again implies that nonviolence is the norm for legitimate response to injustice. But from its reading of history and its interpretation of political experience the just war theory does conclude that some forms of injustice are so serious that they undermine the very possibility of true peace. For example, Pope Paul VI reluctantly left open the possibility of a morally legitimate revolution in conditions of "manifest, long-standing tyranny which would do great damage to fundamental personal rights and dangerous harm to the common good of the country."[14] Thus for just war theory, the goods of peace and justice are interdependent, but justice is regarded as the precondition of peace in the concrete political order. The pursuit of justice, even by force, can in some circumstances be the only way to fulfill the duty to promote both peace and justice.

The ethic of nonviolence rests in part on a similar though less explicit interpretation of the causal interconnection between peace and justice. For pacifism, however, the causal interconnection of the basic values runs in the opposite direction. The priority assigned to justice as a precondition of peace by the just war theory is reversed in the ethics of nonviolence. This view is well expressed in a statement of an American advocate of nonviolence, A. J. Muste: "There is no way to peace, peace is the way."[15]

This pacifist posture is not unconcerned with the pursuit of justice. Activist advocates of nonviolent resistance to injustice are as deeply convinced that nonviolence is the only path to true justice as are just war theorists that a commitment to the pursuit of justice, even by force, is the only path to true peace. The examples of Gandhi, Martin Luther King and many other nonviolent activists provide strong evidence that the commitment to the priority of nonviolence need be neither passive nor ineffective in the face of injustice. Theologians such as John Howard Yoder and James Douglass have argued that the commitment to a nonviolent ethic is the only hope humans have of breaking the "spiral of violence" which breeds further injustice. In their view, to take up arms in the cause of justice is self-defeating.

This argument is often reinforced by a critique of the actual political impact of the just war theory's willingness to legitimate the use of force under certain circumstances. Frederick Russell has pointed out that just war theories have two aims: that of restraining and limiting violence and that of justifying recourse to arms under specified and limited conditions. Which of these aims has in fact been better achieved can be debated. In Russell's view "it remains an open question whether just war theories have limited more wars than they have encouraged."[16] The pacifist reading of the historical impact of just war theory frequently goes one step further than Russell. Gordon Zahn, for example, states that "history makes tragically clear" that military and political decision-makers "will always be ready and eager to exploit every ethical loophole or exception . . . as justification for some new escalation of war's inhumanity."[17] In other words pacifists such as Zahn argue for the priority of nonviolence as a precondition for justice on the basis of both political history and political psychology.

Thus McCormick's claim that the formation of personal and community policies depends on a reading of the way basic values are interrelated seems correct on this level of the pacifist/just war dispute. The problem is evident: the two traditions have differing interpretations of this interrelationship. The argument, however, is more than simply a dispute between persons with different political theories. The pacifist and just war ethics synthesize the conclusions of historical-political interpretation with fundamental religious conviction. The debate, therefore, becomes not only a philosophical or historical-political one but a theological argument about the meaning of the gospel of Jesus Christ and its implications for the political life of the human community.

Chapter 3

Theology and Ethics:
Pluralism "Between the Times"

In determining what scale of value priorities should be adopted in the political and military conflicts of the nuclear age, Christians are pressed to ask some fundamental theological questions about the meaning of their faith in Jesus Christ. Theological reflection is a process of interpretation which illuminates and critiques the taken-for-granted understanding of the human struggle in the light of faith. It also illuminates and critiques our understanding of the reality of the God of Jesus Christ in light of the realities of this human struggle. At the heart of the divergence between the pacifist and just war traditions within the Church lies the basic theological question of how the poles of belief in the gospel and the conclusions of social understanding are to be synthesized with each other.

Just war thinking appeals to the biblical sources of Christian faith to support its political-historical conviction that justice is a precondition for genuine peace. Theologically, the just war position rests on the biblical affirmation that the human community is deeply distorted by human arrogance and sin. Thus conflicts between the demands of justice and the inviolability of human life are not only possible but sadly to be expected. The just war theory presupposes the nonviolent example and teaching of Jesus. On this basis it clearly differs from any approach to warfare which considers the commit-

ment to nonviolence as naive or irrelevant to our actual human conflicts. This difference is evident in the stringent restrictions the theory places on any recourse to force. But just
war theory argues that a *comprehensive* Christian answer to
questions of war and peace must also be based on a full consideration of the central place of the commitment to justice in
biblical faith. It further assumes that the biblical understanding of peace includes justice as one of its essential dimensions.[1]
Thus the theology underlying just war theory synthesizes a
biblical interpretation which is attentive to the nonviolence of
Jesus, to the reality of sin and to the demands of justice with a
historical-political interpretation of the way fundamental values are interrelated. It argues that the pacifist stance not only
absolutizes one human value (human life) at the expense of all
others (justice, freedom, human rights), but also that pacifism
rests on a one-sided reading of the biblical sources.

This theological argument possesses genuine plausibility.
It does not account, however, for one of the central aspects of
the New Testament witness, namely the fact that Jesus did not
resort to violent force in self-defense against unjust attack. Nor
did Jesus counsel the use of violence in the defense of justice
for the Jewish people in the face of Roman oppression. The
theology underlying the pacifist stance on warfare appeals to
these aspects of Jesus' life and death to argue for the religious
and ethical priority of the duty of nonviolence over the duty to
establish justice. It argues that the resort to force contradicts
the strategy for the pursuit of the kingdom of God exemplified
in the life of Jesus. As Edward Schillebeeckx has interpreted
the Scriptures on this question, God's kingdom cannot be
brought about by arms. The force of arms is a sinful obstacle to
the coming of this kingdom:

> The messianic coming of God, before which evil yields, is
> not a coming in power, which will shatter evil with national-
> istic and messianic force of arms. It works through *meta-*
> *noia,* repentance. It is a victory over evil through obedience
> to God, and not through human force. For anyone who
> seeks to achieve a kingdom of peace-without-tears by means

of human force calls Jesus 'a Satan' (Mark 8:27–33 par.; see also Matt 4:1–11; Luke 4:1–13; Mark 1:13). Jesus espouses the cause of redemptive and liberating love, which while not itself disarming and bringing to repentance—on the contrary—nevertheless eventually proves victorious over force. That Beelzebub cannot be driven out by Beelzebub also applies here.... What applies to Jesus in the New Testament applies to all Christians: to follow Jesus to the point of suffering.[2]

Here Schillebeeckx suggests that in the long view nonviolent love is the only effective pathway to the justice of God's kingdom. This theological statement represents a synthesis of the pacifist reading of scripture with its interpretation of the way the human values of peace and justice are interrelated in our historical and political experience. "Beelzebub cannot be driven out by Beelzebub" is seen as a statement that contains both religious and political wisdom.

In the final analysis, however, the pacifist's religious-political commitment to nonviolence as an absolute imperative of the gospel does not base its case on effectiveness in the pursuit of justice within history. Though Yoder and Douglass are activists in the cause of justice, they both acknowledge that effectiveness cannot be the ultimate reason for the absolute priority of nonviolence. Yoder accepts the possibility of a conflict between nonviolence and justice which can be resolved only *outside* of history. When such a conflict occurs, Christians are called to acknowledge that it is God, not they, who holds the ultimate responsibility for establishing the fullness of justice and peace.

This is the deepest meaning of Jesus' willingness to accept an unjust execution rather than take up arms to resist it. As Yoder puts it:

The choice that [Jesus] made in rejecting the crown and accepting the cross was the commitment to such a degree of faithfulness of divine love that he was willing for its sake to sacrifice "effectiveness." Usually it can be argued that from some other perspective or in some long view this renunciation of effectiveness was in fact a very effective thing to do. "If a man will lose his . . . life he shall find it." But this paradoxical possibility does not change the initially solid fact that Jesus thereby excluded any normative concern for any capacity to make sure that things would turn out right.[3]

In other words, the cross of Jesus implies that making things "turn out right" (justice) is subordinate to trust in the God who is the only truly "legitimate authority" in these matters of the ultimate outcome of human history and politics. Gordon Zahn's conclusions about the implications of the Beatitudes and the Sermon on the Mount echo Yoder's understanding of the meaning of the cross:

These, taken in context with the workings of grace and the power of God (which, as Scripture tells us, is made perfect in infirmity), combine to produce an "otherworldly" perspective in which the practice of statecraft becomes at best a secondary consideration. After all, if it avails us not to gain the whole world at the cost of our immortal souls, it might follow that the salvation of our souls could require us to be prepared to suffer the loss of the political and spiritual freedoms we prize where the only alternative is to commit sin.[4]

Zahn, like Yoder and Douglass, is a strong advocate of creative nonviolent action in the defense of these freedoms. Nevertheless, his theology, like pacifist theology in general, is prepared to tolerate injustice in the limit situation where justice cannot be attained by nonviolent means.

The debate between pacifism and just war theory thus presses us to some very fundamental theological questions. Does the commandment to love one's neighbor imply that the incarnation of love in a just social order should take priority over the love of enemies which is expressed in nonviolence? Does the death of Jesus on the cross imply that nonviolent, suffering love is the only authentically Christian response to the reality of injustice? Does the victory of Christ over sin and death in the resurrection imply that Christians are now empowered by God to participate in the shaping of a new and more just earthly society, or is its primary meaning the bestowal of the grace to follow Jesus Christ in the way of the suffering servant? Does Christian hope in the ultimate fulfillment of God's reign of justice and love mean that Christians should look toward that triumph in a spirit of total nonviolence or that they should seek to work toward that fulfillment even through the use of force? The way one answers these religious questions will have a significant impact on how one is disposed to interpret the interconnection between the values of peace and justice in political life. The answers to these questions will also shape one's conclusion about whether the prime Christian responsibility is that of avoiding evil or that of actively pursuing the limited goods which can be achieved in a conflict-ridden world.

These fundamental theological issues need to be explored in much greater depth and in direct relation to the urgent issues of war and peace. A preliminary approach to them can take the following form.

The fullness of God's love revealed in the death and resurrection of Jesus Christ is both model and cause of Christian action for peace and justice. The coming kingdom of God proclaimed by Jesus will be the fulfillment of God's intentions for the whole of creation and for all of humanity. The distortion of God's good creation through the arrogance, duplicity and sloth of humankind means that this fulfillment cannot be achieved without struggle and conflict. The paschal mystery of the life, death and resurrection of Christ is the very embodiment of this struggle between God's reign and the sin of the world. The event of Christ's death and resurrection is the inauguration of that kingdom in which love, justice and the abolition of all violence will be fully accomplished. In the words of the Psalmist, it inaugurates a kingdom in which "kindness and truth shall meet, justice and peace shall kiss" (Ps 85:11, NAB).

It is this paschal mystery as a single unified event which is the basis of Christian hope for the fulfillment of creation through the establishment of justice and the abolition of violence. Neither the crucifixion alone nor the resurrection alone fully presents the content of Christian conviction. The death of Christ on the cross is one aspect of the coming of the kingdom of God. It shows that this coming entails both conflict and self-sacrifice. But the Father's act of raising Jesus from the dead is a second and equally significant aspect of the paschal event. The resurrection of Christ is the victory of God's love over the power of sin and the inauguration of the reign of God's justice for the human race.

The resurrection shows humanity that the ultimate intention of the God of love is the establishment of the fullness of mutual union of all persons with God and with each other. Though the crucifixion implies that there can be no victory over sin without struggle and self-sacrifice, the resurrection and sending of the Holy Spirit tell us that God's will for humanity is the communion of person with person in truly mutual bondedness—a communion which has equality and justice as one of its essential prerequisites. Though Christian love, modeled on and rooted in the paschal mystery, can call for self-sacrifice, it is only realized fully in mutual union and in the equal regard of persons for each other which is the root meaning of justice.[5] And as Margaret Farley has stated, this mutuality between persons which is promised by the resurrection "does not merely beckon from the future; it continually impinges upon the present, demanding that every relationship . . . be at least turned in the direction of equality and opened to the possibility of communion."[6] Thus the paschal mystery calls Christians to an active pursuit of the justice which is the precondition for the mutual communion of the kingdom of God.

Therefore, in shaping their lives in history, Christians are compelled to look back to the cross and resurrection of Christ and to see in this event a call to both nonviolence and justice. At the same time they are compelled to look forward to the kingdom whose realization will establish the fullness of love and justice in the relations between all persons and God and which will abolish violence forever. However in the time between the paschal event which forms Christian memory and

kingdom which is the object of Christian hope an unresolved
tension between justice and nonviolence continues to exist.
This tension can never be fully overcome within history. The
total reconciliation of justice and peace is an eschatological
reality. Within time the imperatives of justice and the demands of nonviolence can and sometimes do conflict. But
neither of these fundamental values can be regarded as less
important from a Christian theological perspective.

This implies, I believe, that *both* the pacifist commitment
to nonviolence and self-sacrifice as the way to justice and the
just war tradition's commitment to justice as the way to peace
and mutual love are essential if the full content of Christian
hope is to be made visible in history. Each of these ethical
stances bears witness to an essential part of the Christian
mystery. Each of them, however, is incomplete by itself. Within time it is simply not possible to embody the fullness of the
kingdom of God in a single form of life or a single ethical
standard. Thus if the Christian community is to be faithful to
the full meaning of the paschal mystery as the inauguration of
the kingdom of God, there must be a pluralism of ethical
stances represented within it. I would conclude, therefore,
that both the pacifist ethic and the just war ethic are legitimate
and necessary expressions of the Christian faith. The necessity
for such pluralism in approaching the morality of warfare is a
particular case of the more general theological truth that the
kingdom of God cannot be fully expressed in any single historical way of living or hierarchy of basic values. Pacifism and just
war theory are both historical syntheses of a particular aspect
of the Christian hope with an historical-political interpretation
of how the basic values of justice and peace are related to each
other within time. The fact that these two traditions have been
present within the Christian community for millennia has not
been an accident but a theological necessity. This conclusion
should not be interpreted as the expression of a desire not to
offend either camp. It is intended as a theological statement
about the reality of the Christian life "between the times" of
the inauguration of the kingdom and its eschatological fulfillment. A pluralism of responses to the question of whether

nonviolence or justice is primary in a Christian ethic is not just a sociological fact. It is the theological consequence of the incompleteness and partiality of *any* specification of the relation between the kingdom of God and the realities of history.

At the same time it is important to note that this argument for pluralism does not mean that the Christian community as a whole is at liberty to adopt either of the two ethical stances in an exclusive way. *Both* of these ethical positions must be present within the Church if it is to be faithful to the full reality of Jesus Christ. As James Childress has put it: "Pacifists and proponents of just war theories really need each other."[7] Those who use just war theory in addressing the nuclear question need the pacifist witness to the centrality of nonviolence. They need this to prevent them from losing their memory of the original just war question as they engage in the intricate analyses of the relation between just war norms and the complexities of current policy debates. Pacifists need the continual reminder of the centrality of justice in the Christian vision which the just war theory provides. In addition they need to be pressed never to forget that Christian responsibility extends beyond the avoidance of evil to the positive promotion of both justice and peace. While the temptation of just war theorists is that of too quickly legitimating violence, pacifists can be tempted to acquiesce in the face of injustice too quickly. Similarly, just war thinkers are often in danger of losing their moral bearings as they engage in the intricacies of political and military analysis, while pacifists risk removing themselves from these policy debates altogether. Though on some questions Christians might be justified in withdrawing from careful debate about the details of public policy, this can surely not be the case where hundreds of millions of lives are at stake. Pacifists and just war thinkers need each other to keep the Christian community as a whole engaged in shaping these policies in ways that accord with the demands of both justice and peace.

This conclusion, then, sees the two ethical stances as complementary and interconnected for both theological, ecclesiological and psychosocial reasons. McCormick's notion of the interconnectedness of basic values can be carried a step further to argue for an interconnected complementarity of basic ethical postures. No one person can be both a pacifist and a just war thinker. But individual Christians can and must be committed to both peace and justice. The precise stance of an individual person will be a function of personal vocation and level of responsibility for the political decisions which nations must make when faced with violent threats or aggression. Also, each of these stances can be supported by solid theological reasoning and by plausible historical-political interpretations of human experience. As the Christian community seeks to address questions of nuclear policy, it must rely on both of these sub-traditions to shape its corporate response in the light of both faith and political wisdom.

Part Two

Policies:
Fighting and Deterring
Nuclear War

Chapter 4

Criteria for Policy Evaluation

The first part of this essay has argued for the legitimacy of a pluralism of basic moral stances toward the morality of warfare. Both the ethic of nonviolence and the just war ethic embody partial and complementary insights into the implications of Christian faith for our life in history and political society. This pluralism, however, is not infinitely expansible. Nor is it compatible with all possible policies governing the use of force. Legitimate pluralism extends as far as the boundaries of reasonable disagreement about the interrelation of the values of justice and peace, and only this far. Diversity in the interpretation of the way these values are interconnected is possible on both the historical-political and the theological levels. But the limits of pluralism cannot be stretched to permit support for policies which transgress the norms of the just war theory. The just war doctrine does not legitimate any and every use of violence. Together with pacifism it shares the conviction that human agents are under a genuine obligation to avoid injury or violence to other human beings. It diverges from pacifism in its conclusion that this obligation is not an absolute one. The criteria of the just war theory set down the conditions under which *exceptions* to the general obligation of nonviolence might be made. As a theory of *exceptions,* it marks the outside limit for pluralism in the evaluation of the morality of warfare. Christian ethics cannot insist that pacifism is an obligatory stance for all persons and nations for the theological reasons sketched above. It can insist, however, that force which violates the just war norms is never legitimate.

The just war limit to the scope of moral pluralism is crucial in forming the Christian community's corporate contribution to the public debate about nuclear weapons policies. It may be impossible to find a single normative framework for the evaluation of warfare which gives historical expression to the full justice and peace of the kingdom of God. But this does not mean that anything goes or that all is fair in modern warfare. The limits on legitimate pluralism within the Church concerning basic moral perspectives on warfare imply that there are moral limits on warfare itself.

The criteria which state these outside limits will be outlined in this chapter. These criteria are the norms of the just war theory. The just war norms do not embody the only Christian approach to warfare. They do, however, hold a privileged place in the Christian community's effort to make a contribution to the formation of public policy. The privileged place of just war norms in policy debate is an implication of theologically legitimate pluralism. Christians could insist that policies be formed on a pacifist foundation only if theological and historical-political argument could establish that the pacifist stance were mandatory for all persons and societies. Pacifist convictions can and should be protected through legislation guaranteeing the right of conscientious objection. But public policy in a pluralist society cannot be held to norms for the use of force which are more stringent than those of the just war theory. To do so would be to deny the legitimate plurality of approaches we have argued for.

The just war tradition has developed a refined set of moral categories for reasoning about the possible justification of violence in the pursuit of justice. These categories have been formulated in different ways during different phases of the tradition, but in this context they can be summarized briefly. The criteria fall into two broad groups. *Jus ad bellum* criteria determine whether the alleged grounds for the initiation of armed hostilities are sufficiently grave to override the *prima facie* obligation of nonviolence. *Jus in bello* norms govern the judgment regarding the use of particular means within war. *Ad bellum* norms include the following:

1. *Legitimate authority.* This criterion states that resort to arms is not a private prerogative of individuals. The ordinary social instrument for the enforcement of justice is a legitimately constituted government. This criterion submits the decision to resort to force in the pursuit of justice to the ordinary criteria of political legitimacy. In cases of revolutionary insurrection, where the government has lost its legitimacy through persistent disregard for justice and violation of the human rights of its citizens, this authority may transfer to extragovernmental movements.

2. *Just cause.* The use of force can only be for the protection of justice. It cannot be for the sake of vengeance or domination. Both in contemporary international law and in Roman Catholic thought since Pope Pius XII it has been further argued that the ferocity and destructiveness of modern war make it necessary to limit the use of force to a defense against injustice. Aggressive wars, even in the cause of justice, are regarded as so likely to unleash total war as to make them incompatible with justice itself. Such aggressive, or self-initiated, uses of force are also judged to be serious obstacles to the creation of the international institutions of world order which are prerequisites for genuine justice in the modern world. Thus the only just cause is defense against unjust attack.[1]

3. *Last resort.* This criterion is an evident corollary to the *prima facie* obligation not to injure human beings. If defense against injustice can be achieved by means other than force there is a moral obligation to use these nonviolent means. Thus all peaceful alternatives to the use of force must have been exhausted before force can be justified. These peaceful means include bilateral negotiations and full employment of regional and international mechanisms for conflict resolution.

4. *Need for a declaration of war.* This criterion is problematic given the speed with which international events can unfold in our world. However, the point of the criterion remains highly relevant. Force should not be used unless a potential adversary has been given every opportunity to

change the course of events and unless there has been an opportunity for serious political debate and consent by the citizens of the defending country or their representatives.

5. *Proportionality.* This criterion states that the values of justice to be defended by force must be so great as to outweigh the harms which necessarily accompany any use of force. Conversely, it also implies that the force employed must do no greater harm than the evil which is resisted. Furthermore, as William O'Brien has pointed out, "the balance sheet of good and evil must be estimated for each belligerent. Additionally, there should be a balancing of effects on individual third parties and on the international common good. International interdependence means that international conflicts are difficult to contain and that their shock waves affect third parties in a manner that must be accounted for in the calculus of probable good and evil."[2] The judgment of proportionality must weigh all the effects which can be expected to flow from hostilities. A large amount of political wisdom is necessarily called for in making such an estimate. Pacifists and just war thinkers can both defend their stances by presenting plausible interpretations of the overall consequences of any use of force in the contemporary world and by backing up these interpretations with theological arguments. Nevertheless it is quite possible for them to agree that the criterion of proportionality sets the outside limit for any *possible* justification of force in a world where fundamental values conflict.

6. *Reasonable hope of success.* This criterion is a further specification of the norm of proportionality. It recognizes that judgments of proportion between the good and evil effects of warfare are *estimates* of the possible or probable outcomes of action. There is a greater or lesser element of uncertainty in all such estimates. The criterion calls for a *reasonable* assurance that the good of justice will be achieved and a *reasonable* conviction that the last state of the belligerents and other affected parties will not be worse than the first. The application of this criterion again calls for political prudence and practical wisdom. It implies, however, that the uncertainty inherent in warfare of any kind cannot be used to argue that

the use of force is justified because we do not *know* that its outcome will be disproportionate. Given the presumptions against violence that both pacifism and just war theory share, we need as a *minimum* a reasonable confidence that the outcome *will* be proportionate. As will become clear below, this criterion is of great importance in the moral evaluation of policies governing the use of nuclear weapons.

7. *Right intention.* Since the only cause which can justify resort to force is the defense of justice, the intention of a belligerent must be limited to this end. Intention here does not refer to the psychological states of the parties in conflict. Rather it concerns the purposes or ends which they are seeking through the use of force.[3] The only purpose which can be legitimately pursued by the use of force is the defense of justice and the genuine peace whose precondition is justice. Thus the requirement of right intention places limits on the purposes for which force may be employed. It may not be used in order to achieve domination over another nation, for such a goal is itself unjust. It may not be used for purposes of vengeance, for revenge does nothing to establish justice. It must not be used in a way which makes attainment of a just peace unattainable. All of these aspects of right intention show how the *prima facie* obligation to nonviolence and non-injury continues to make a claim on conscience even when they are judged less stringent than the claims of justice.[4]

The *jus in bello* norms of the just war theory set moral limits on the means that may be used even in a conflict which is itself justified under *ad bellum* criteria. The fundamental principle behind the *in bello* criteria is the conviction that total or all-out violence is never justified. As William O'Brien has put it, "The single, underlying requirement for the conduct of just war is that such a war must be limited. Unlimited war is never just, no matter how important the just cause."[5] The criteria which specify these limits are two.

1. *Discrimination.* This norm states that non-combatants must be immune from direct attack. The basis of this criterion is the fundamental conviction shared by both pacifism and just war theory that human life is sacred and that we have a

genuine obligation to protect it. Pacifism raises this conviction to the level of an absolute, while just war theory regretfully concludes that some acts of killing are justified. But the direct killing of persons who are in no way a threat to other human lives or to fundamental goods such as justice or human rights can never be approved. In other words, the direct killing of non-combatants is murder.[6]

2. *Proportionality.* Like the *ad bellum* criterion of proportionality, *in bello* proportionality demands that the harm caused by a particular military means must be outweighed by the value that it can reasonably be expected to protect. It is important to note, however, that this judgment of proportion does not balance the harm caused by a particular tactic against the good being defended by the war as a whole. Such an interpretation of *in bello* proportionality would remove all restraint from the use of force in defense of a just cause. It leads to what Michael Walzer, following General Sherman, has called the "War is hell" doctrine. According to this unacceptable way of judging proportionality, "war is entirely and singularly the crime of those who begin it, and soldiers resisting aggression (or rebellion) can never be blamed for anything they do that brings victory closer."[7] Correctly understood, *in bello* proportionality weighs the harm caused by a tactic in a just war against the tactical advantages gained by this means. Thus, for example, the Allied saturation bombing of Dresden in World War II not only violated the *in bello* norm of discrimination. It also transgressed *in bello* proportionality, for there was no comparability between the military value of this tactic and the destruction it caused.[8] *In bello* proportionality, therefore, can only justify the use of *limited* military means for the pursuit of *limited* military objectives. If either of these limits is abandoned, war becomes total and, *eo ipso*, unjust. For in total war the *prima facie* obligation of non-injury is not merely overridden in the defense of other values, it is denied outright and rendered irrelevant to moral decision-making.

All these criteria of the just war theory express a single basic conviction: force is at best a marginally defensible instrument for the pursuit of justice. The criteria do not rest simply on a conclusion about the relative stringency of our obligations to nonviolence and to the protection of justice. Were the just war theory based solely on a conclusion that justice is a more important human value than nonviolence, then the use of violence would be justified whenever the cause is just. Rather, the just war norms arise from a consideration of how the basic values of life, freedom, justice, etc. are related to each other in the light of our historical experience and our practical understanding of the functioning of the political order. They are norms of political morality, and as such they are a synthesis of both political judgment and moral commitment. Further, as Stanley Hoffmann has observed, "All ethical judgments in politics, but especially judgments in this field, are historical judgments."[9] The just war criteria embody a representative tradition of Christian and humanist practical wisdom. They encapsulate the historical experience of the West concerning the restrictions which must be placed on the use of force if it is to be limited to the protection of justice as the basis of a genuine peace.

Because these criteria are rooted in historical-political judgment as well as in moral conviction, they are subject to revision in light of changes in our historical and political experience. The pacifist tradition in Christian ethics argues the non-theological part of its case against the just war on a competing historical-political interpretation of the relation between nonviolence and justice. It maintains that the use of force inevitably contributes to an escalating spiral of both violence and injustice. The pacifist theological argument from the death of Jesus Christ on the cross to an absolute obligation of nonviolence cannot be made the basis for a political ethic for a pluralist society. But the historical-political aspect of the pacifist case deserves to be fully considered in the effort to elaborate norms for public policy in the nuclear age. For the advent of nuclear technologies has given new weight to the pacifist argument that the use of force cannot be expected to serve the cause of either justice or peace. In other words, nuclear weapons have introduced a qualitatively new reality into our historical and political experience—a reality which may call for a revision of the just war theory's willingness to legitimate some limited used of force. In arguing this question of the appropriate norms for public policy, just war theory and pacifism may be able to overcome their differences and reach a new consensus on the practical, if not the theological, level. The possibility of such a consensus depends on the willingness of both groups to bring all the resources of human intelligence and understanding to bear on the political and military realities of the nuclear age. In other words, beginning from different theological starting points the two sub-traditions of Christian thought may converge on the common ground of contemporary historical-political policy judgment. Though just war theory is the most stringent normative framework that can be proposed for policy, the pacifist perspective on the historical record of the use of violence has new relevance in our historical moment. Just war theory needs this perspective if it is to employ its own insights in the nuclear era.

The key to the formation of a just war/pacifist consensus on nuclear policy is the fact that both groups are in agreement that the present realities of the nuclear age have brought with them a qualitatively new potential for both murderous violence and profound injustice. Both the growth of pacifism and the renewal of just war analysis within the Church in recent years have in large measure been a response to the ominous threat posed by nuclear weapons. In discussing this threat in his encyclical letter *Pacem in Terris,* Pope John XXIII stated that "in an age such as ours, which prides itself on its atomic energy, it is contrary to reason to hold that war is now a suitable way to restore rights which have been violated."[10] In the context of a similar discussion, the Second Vatican Council referred to "the massive and indiscriminate destruction" which modern scientific weapons are capable of inflicting.[11] The Council then went on to state, "all these considerations compel us to undertake an evaluation of war with an entirely new attitude."[12] The theme of the morally problematic character of warfare in the nuclear age was reiterated most recently by Pope John Paul II in his homily at Coventry Cathedral in Great Britain: "Today, the scale and the horror of modern warfare—whether nuclear or not—makes it totally unacceptable as a means of settling differences between nations. War should belong to the tragic past, to history; it should find no place on humanity's agenda for the future."[13]

Bryan Hehir has pointed out that papal and conciliar statements such as these are open to various interpretations when placed in the context from which they have been drawn.[14] James Douglass, for example, appears to believe that the nuclear age is leading the Church to a pacifist position through a two-step evolution of thought which is not yet complete. First, Douglass acknowledges that the prime concern of just war theory is the pursuit of justice, not the legitimation of war. He argues, however, that in the nuclear age it is becoming apparent that violent force is not in fact compatible with the attainment of justice:

> Always implicit [in just war theory] is the assumption that the waging of war can sometimes be consistent with the attainment of such justice. If, as a result of weapons developments which St. Augustine could hardly have foreseen, war and justice should be seen to have reached an absolute conflict, war as the physical factor in the theory must give way to justice as the ruling moral principle.[15]

This conflict between modern war and justice is the basis of the contemporary argument that even on just war grounds Christians are obligated to adopt a stance of nuclear pacifism. The nuclear pacifist maintains that all use of nuclear weapons fails the test of the just war criteria, or, in stronger form, that in a nuclear-armed world no war can withstand scrutiny according to these norms.

The second step in the evolution that Douglass believes is underway in Church teachings on warfare is a move from nuclear pacifism to an absolute commitment to nonviolence. He believes that this step was implicitly taken by John XXIII in *Pacem in Terris,* and is the logical outcome of Vatican II's call to "undertake an evaluation of war with an entirely new attitude."[16] For Douglass, the threats of the nuclear age are

leading the Church to recover an insight it should never have
lost: the absolute obligation of nonviolence. As Bryan Hehir
has observed, Douglass's argument for the presence of the
second of these developments in Church teaching goes beyond
the evidence. Vatican II and John Paul II have both reiterated
the existence of "the right to legitimate defense once every
means of peaceful settlement has been exhausted."[17] Also, as
has been argued above, it would seem that an *exclusive* commitment by the Church to nonviolence would go beyond the
theological possibilities of our existence "between the times."
Though the problems which beset any attempt to set moral
limits to revolutionary warfare are enormous, it does not seem
that pacifists and just war thinkers are ready to come to agreement in this area.[18] However, there is a much stronger basis
for the hope that agreement can be reached on the question of
the morality of the use of nuclear weapons. To that policy
question we now turn, with both the just war and pacifist
interpretations of the relation of justice and peace fully in
mind.

Chapter 5

The Use of Nuclear Weapons

The question of whether the use of nuclear weapons can ever be a morally legitimate instrument of justice has not been clearly addressed in recent Church teaching. Nor has a clear consensus on this question been achieved by moral theologians. It is an issue which has become one of the chief foci in the continuing debate over nuclear strategy in the United States today.

For the pacifist the answer to this question is clear and unambiguous. Since all use of lethal force is judged to be incompatible with the gospel, then *a fortiori* the use of nuclear weapons must be rejected. The answer is equally evident to just war thinkers who adopt what John Langan has called "the absolutist approach to applying the criteria of just war theory to the possibility of nuclear war."[1] Those who adopt this approach conclude to an absolute moral prohibition on the use of nuclear weapons on just war grounds. They reach this conclusion by arguing that nuclear weapons are weapons of mass destruction which are necessarily indiscriminate. Their use is judged greater than necessary to repel an enemy attack. And the harm they would cause is disproportionate to any good attainable by their use.[2] Langan agrees that if these arguments are valid, then the absolute moral prohibition against using nuclear weapons must follow.

Langan also argues, however, that the clear immorality of some uses of nuclear weapons does not necessarily lead to the conclusion that all uses will exceed just war limits. "We must remember the burden of proof that a proponent of the basic premise of the absolutist argument is assuming. What this requires is that one show that *every* instance of using a nuclear weapon is wrong, that it is an exercise of force which produces unjustifiable harm."[3] In other words, Langan calls for the identification of the multiple ways that nuclear weapons might be employed in warfare and an evaluation of each of these possible uses on its own merits. He rejects any a priori evaluation of these different strategies *en bloc*.

Langan's point is a good one. But his willingness to leave open the possibility of some legitimate uses of nuclear weapons can be questioned. First, he places the burden of proof on those who argue that the use of these weapons is unjustified. In fact, the whole structure of the just war theory would place the burden of proof on those who declare that any use of these weapons is justifiable. Langan observes that the absolute prohibition on use seems particularly appealing "to those who have, in a real though often disguised way, opted for pacifism."[4] It would be more accurate to state that the absolute prohibition is more likely to be appealing to those who have not forgotten the intent of the original just war question and where it locates the burden of proof. Just war theory presupposes that resort to force is illegitimate. It is justified only by way of exception.

Second, Langan argues against an a priori approach to the morality of use and for a consideration of possible uses on a case by case basis. Nevertheless he does not in fact analyze the uses of nuclear weapons he thinks may be justified in their concrete political and military contexts. Rather, he refers to "hypothetical cases in which nuclear weapons are used against military targets in a way which does not produce disproportional collateral damage and which does not involve direct attacks on non-combatants."[5] The question is not whether such hypotheses can be constructed, but whether they can ever be realized in actual situations of contemporary warfare. Langan's argument is a useful challenge to those who form their conclusions about the use of nuclear weapons solely from a consideration of the effects of all-out employment. But we need more detailed scrutiny of the actual historical possibilities than are provided by Langan. Accepting Langan's appeal to avoid a priori reasoning about the use of nuclear weapons, we must examine different strategies for their use that have actually been proposed by policy makers.

The most horrendous of these possibilities—a direct nuclear attack upon population centers of another nation—patently fails to meet the just war criteria. Such an attack involves the intended killing of vast numbers of non-combatants. It therefore falls under Vatican II's often-quoted condemnation of indiscriminate bombing:

> Any act of war aimed indiscriminately at the destruction of entire cities or of extensive areas along with their population is a crime against God and man himself. It merits unequivocal and unhesitating condemnation.[6]

This *in bello* norm of discrimination applies to counter-city attacks whether they be offensive or in retaliation. This conclusion is reinforced by other just war criteria, particularly that of proportionality, for once counter-city warfare has begun it is very likely to lead to an all-out mutual exchange resulting in the destruction of all those values which might make more limited forms of warfare sometimes marginally justifiable. Thus counter-city warfare also violates the criterion of reasonable hope of success. Even if one argues with William V. O'Brien[7] that non-combatant immunity is a goal to be pursued to the fullest extent possible rather than an imperative which is always binding, the likelihood of escalation places counter-city attacks beyond the bounds of rational action.

O'Brien has argued that proportionality is a more fundamental norm than is non-combatant immunity. In light of this argument he has concluded that counter-city attacks might be justified for one purpose and one purpose alone: "Selective strategic countervalue attacks carried on to deter a continuation of antecedent selective countervalue attacks by the aggressor could be justified."[8] O'Brien's argument is essentially the following: one country could selectively "take out" cities of a nuclear aggressor in order to convince the aggressor to do no further damage to the population of the defending country. He is able to reach this conclusion, based on proportionality, only by sidestepping the dangers of escalation and the criterion of reasonable hope of success.[9]

As a number of historians of just war theory have shown, the criterion of non-combatant immunity is a rather late development in this tradition.[10] But these historians of the tradition also have shown that non-combatant immunity has come to the fore in latter-day just war analysis precisely because of the increasingly evident disproportion of any war which violates it.[11] In the case of counter-city nuclear attacks, the disproportion between civilian deaths and reasonable military objectives threatens, with high probability, to become total. Thus I would conclude that we have learned something from historical experience that reinforces the Christian conviction that love of neighbor implies that force may only be directed against persons who participate in the perpetration of injustice.[12] Whole cities are never legitimate military targets for any reason or in any circumstance.

Langan is in agreement with this conclusion, for he holds the principle of non-combatant immunity. His challenge to the "absolutist" proscription of all use of nuclear weapons is based on other proposals for their possible use. The contemporary debates about nuclear policy raise issues which call for a more complex form of moral reflection than that required by counter-city warfare. Some U.S. defense analysts advocate policies which envision the limited use of strategic nuclear weapons against the military forces, command-control-and-communication systems, political and bureaucratic leadership, and key economic resources of the adversary. These strategic scenarios plan for the use of nuclear weapons by one superpower against the homeland of the other. Their primary targets, however, are not population centers as such but military forces and the political and economic structures necessary for the conduct of hostilities.

These limited strategic counterforce scenarios therefore give the appearance of coming closer to meeting the *in bello* criteria of discrimination and proportionality.[13] But this appearance is deceptive for several reasons. In August of 1980 at the Naval War College, Secretary of Defense Harold Brown outlined the basic premises of the United States' strategic planning as contained in the classified document known as Presidential Directive 59. The premises of the "countervailing strategy" contained in the Directive include a new emphasis on selective use of nuclear weapons against targets which are of military and political significance. But neither P.D. 59 nor subsequent refinements of its basic strategic approach[14] have eliminated the potential use of nuclear weapons against cities. As Secretary Brown stated:

> Operationally, our countervailing strategy requires that our plans and capabilities be structured to put more stress on being able to employ strategic nuclear forces selectively as well as by all-out retaliation in response to massive attacks on the United States. It is our policy—and we have increasingly the means and the detailed plans to carry out this policy—to insure that the Soviet leadership knows that if they chose some intermediate level of aggression, we could, by selection of large but still less than maximum nuclear attacks, exact an unacceptably high price in the things that the Soviet leaders appear to value most—political and military control, military force both nuclear and conventional and the industrial capacity to sustain a war.

> ... And, of course, we have and will keep a survivable and enduring capability to attack the full range of targets, including the Soviet economic base, if that is the appropriate response to a Soviet strike.[15]

From this statement it is clear that the countervailing strategy contained in P.D. 59 seeks to provide an alternative other than surrender or all-out war should the United States be attacked with nuclear weapons by the U.S.S.R. It is also clear that the strategy leaves open the possibility of attack on "the full range of targets" should limited war fail to achieve its goals.

The countervailing strategy of P.D. 59 and its subsequent

refinements can therefore be challenged on a number of grounds. First, these war-fighting strategies do not eliminate the technical means for counter-city warfare nor have they removed cities from the list of potential targets. Second, the argument for the moral superiority of strategic counterforce strategies rests on the supposition that the use of nuclear weapons can be kept limited to military targets. This supposition can be questioned. In the eyes of the leaders of a nation whose military forces are being attacked by strategic weapons, the effects of these attacks will be exceedingly difficult to distinguish from an attack on cities. The collateral damage to the population if military and political targets in urban areas are struck would look much like the results of a direct attack on these cities. In addition, the use of strategic nuclear weapons is likely to damage the command-control-and-communication systems of the attacked nation so seriously that leaders will find it difficult or impossible to know what the adversary's intentions and actions really are.[16] Further, if the political leadership of either superpower were attacked, as the countervailing strategy envisions, the result would be "nuclear decapitation." Lacking a central command structure, the use of strategic nuclear forces by both superpowers could quickly escape rational control.[17] Even more ominously, the political control necessary to negotiate the cessation of hostilities would be absent. Thus collateral damage, command-control-and-communication vulnerability, and loss of the structures of centralized political decision making all exert powerful pressure for escalation to mutual destruction. As Keeny and Panofsky have observed, there is an "almost inevitable link between any use of nuclear weapons and the grim 'mutual hostage' realities of the MAD world."[18] The use of any strategic nuclear weapons increases the likelihood of massive counter-city attacks.

Thus, a key element in the dispute over whether strategic counterforce war-fighting strategies are morally less objectionable than are strategies which envision the destruction of cities is the prudential military-political judgment about whether the limitation of nuclear war can indeed be predicted with any reasonable amount of confidence. U.S. Department of Defense policy statements acknowledge that any employment of strategic nuclear weapons by one superpower against the other can be expected to escalate rapidly into an all-out war.[19] No one can be sure of the outcome of an attempt to conduct limited nuclear war directed against the military and political structure of a nation which itself possesses nuclear weapons. But the bulk of the strategic literature on this question and most of the public statements of the national leaders of the countries involved imply that it is highly unlikely that such limits would be respected.

The *ad bellum* criterion of reasonable hope of success becomes the relevant moral norm in this debate. In my view, the hope that any use of strategic weapons can be kept limited exceeds the bounds of reasonable judgment. A policy which aims at the actual use of strategic weapons against the other superpower's forces must thus be judged unacceptable as an instrument for the pursuit of goals which are themselves just. In my judgment, this conclusion applies not only to the initiation of a limited nuclear exchange, but also to strategic retaliation as well. To respond to a nuclear attack on one's own military forces by launching strategic nuclear weapons against the forces of the attacking nation increases the probability of escalation to the point of mass slaughter. Therefore the use of strategic nuclear weapons even in would-be limited wars must be judged morally unjustifiable on the grounds of both *ad bellum* and *in bello* norms. This conclusion goes beyond the explicit teachings of the Holy See, though it has been supported by a number of ethical writings and episcopal statements.[20] I believe it should become a firm judgment of the developing Christian consensus on the morality of nuclear warfare.

The current debate on nuclear strategy has also focused on the possibility of another form of limited nuclear war: that involving the use of intermediate range or tactical nuclear weapons in the defense of Western Europe. Here again, the moral judgment about such scenarios is dependent upon a military-political judgment about the actual likelihood of keeping such use limited. A significant debate on this point has begun in recent months in the journal *Foreign Affairs*. In their important essay urging the adoption of a policy of "no first use" of nuclear weapons by the North Atlantic Alliance, McGeorge Bundy, George F. Kennan, Robert S. McNamara and Gerard Smith propose a reexamination of the overall structure of NATO defense and deterrence strategy. In the course of their discussion of this complex area, they affirm that the profusion of nuclear weapons systems in Europe on both sides of the East/West boundary "has made it more difficult than ever to construct rational plans for any first use of these weapons by anyone."[21] They then go on to state an even stronger conclusion:

> It is time to recognize that no one has ever succeeded in advancing any persuasive reason to believe that any use of nuclear weapons, even on the smallest scale, could reliably be expected to remain limited. Every serious analysis and every military exercise, for over 25 years, have demonstrated that even the most restrained battlefield use would be enormously destructive to civilian life and property. There is no way for anyone to have any confidence that such a nuclear action will not lead to further and more devastating exchanges. Any use of nuclear weapons in Europe, by the Alliance or against it, carries with it a high and inescapable risk of escalation into the general nuclear war which would bring ruin to all and victory to none.[22]

A number of the published responses to the Bundy-Kennan-McNamara-Smith essay have been critical of the authors' proposal.[23] Most of these critical responses base their objections on the grounds that a "no first use" policy would weaken the Western deterrent against Warsaw Pact aggression. We will deal with the deterrence issue in the following chapter. In the context of the present discussion of the morality of the use of nuclear weapons, it is important to note that the critics of the proposal made by Bundy *et al.* do not respond to the fundamental assertion that it is highly improbable that a nuclear exchange could actually be kept limited once any use had in fact occurred. The authors of the original essay have taken note of this fact:

> In all the comment and criticism our essay has received there has not been one concrete suggestion as to just how a first use of nuclear weapons would be carried out—in which numbers and with what targets. We think there is a reason for this reticence. All the specific proposals we have encountered over the years, and they have been many, look unacceptably dangerous in the context of the forces now deployed on both sides.[24]

The dangers of first use which are emphasized here by the authors are also present in the case of retaliatory use of nuclear weapons in the European theater. The likelihood of escalation to general nuclear war which attends *any* use of nuclear weapons in Europe makes such use an irrational means to the pursuit even of such legitimate values as freedom and justice. This irrationality is not the result of a failure to design sufficiently sophisticated strategies or more precise weapons systems. Rather, it follows from the dangers of escalation which attend any crossing of the nuclear threshold. Langan has proposed hypothetical cases in which tactical nuclear weapons might be used in Europe which are compatible with just war norms. He acknowledges, however, that "such proposed cases fail to allay our anxieties about the likely consequences of resorting to nuclear weapons; for we cannot know that the reality ahead of us will conform to our cases and scenarios."[25] When we begin to think about concrete rather than hypothetical cases, it becomes clear that these anxieties are quite well founded.

I would therefore conclude on the basis of a combination of the *in bello* criteria of discrimination and proportionality and the *ad bellum* criterion of reasonable hope of success that no use of nuclear weapons in Europe can be justified.

An additional consideration about the moral aspects of strategies for fighting limited nuclear wars concerns the moral legitimacy of "collateral damage" to civilian populations which would accompany nuclear attacks on military targets. The traditional *in bello* criterion of discrimination rules out *direct* attacks on non-combatants. Consequently, some participants in the current public argument have concluded that the deaths of civilians caused by strategic or tactical nuclear attacks on military targets do not violate the norm of discrimination.

In contemporary Catholic moral theology, there has been an intense dispute about the significance of the direct/indirect distinction.[26] This debate is important in itself and the way it is resolved is relevant to the way one reasons about the morality of collateral damage to civilian populations. Nevertheless, I believe that proponents of the different positions in this debate should reach the same conclusion about the issue at hand. Those on one side of the debate hold that the directly intended object of a counterforce attack is the destruction of a military target and that civilian deaths are unintended indirect consequences. According to this view one is still bound, by the traditional interpretation of the principle of double effect, to weigh the evil consequences which indirectly accompany the attack against the good effects which flow from it. In other words, it is not enough that civilian deaths be unintended. There must also be a proportionality between this loss of life and the military purposes which the attack seeks to achieve. As Langan has rightly observed, "large-scale hostilities in central Europe are very likely to produce unacceptable levels of civilian casualties, whether conventional or nuclear forces are employed. This creates problems about non-combatant losses, collateral damage, and proportionality well before one gets to the question of nuclear escalation."[27] The same is true of strategic counterforce attacks against the homelands of the superpowers, especially since political leadership and industrial capacity are included as "counterforce" targets. When one includes, as one must, the dangers of escalation of either strategic attacks or the use of nuclear weapons in the European theater, the disproportion becomes even more evident. Thus on the basis of traditional double-effect analysis, the claim that collateral damage is indirectly intended provides no justification for the employment of nuclear weapons. As Michael Walzer has put it:

> The collateral damage likely to be caused by a "legitimate" use of nuclear weapons is so great that it would violate both of the proportionality limits fixed by the theory of war: the number of people killed in the war as a whole would not be warranted by the goals of the war—particularly since the dead would include many if not most of the people for whose defense the war was being fought; and the number of people killed in individual actions would be disproportionate (under the doctrine of double effect) to the value of the military targets directly attacked.[28]

This conclusion about the disproportionality of collateral damage depends on a judgment of the likely effects of the use of nuclear weapons. It is only by prescinding from the concrete conditions under which nuclear weapons might be used that some theologians have been willing to see collateral damage as possibly justified.[29] Such an approach is insufficiently attentive to military, geographical and political realities.

The other school of moral theologians in the debate about the distinction between direct and indirect intention approaches the question of collateral damage in a somewhat different way. This school of thought, which is frequently called consequentialism or proportionalism, argues that one cannot determine what an agent intends to do without considering the consequences which the agent foresees will follow from the contemplated action. If an agent chooses to perform an action whose good consequences are reasonably judged to be greater than are its evil consequences, this second school would judge that the intention is a morally upright one. On the other hand, if the foreseen evil consequences are proportionately greater, then the direct object of the intention is evil. This would be the case, for example, if one could foresee that a nuclear attack on a military target would produce a level of civilian deaths and environmental damage which outweighs the projected contribution to the protection of human life and the defense of justice.

In making such judgments the problem of the incommensurability of basic human values raised by Grisez, Finnis and Ramsey comes center stage once again. For example, if one is fighting for the physical and cultural survival of Western civilization then it might appear that extremely large amounts of collateral damage from strikes on military targets would be justified. Grisez *et al.* would rightly protest against such weighing of the consequences of a particular military tactic against all the values embodied in our culture. This kind of weighing would be indistinguishable from General Sherman's "War is hell" doctrine. But the contemporary consequentialist or proportionalist argument within moral theology does not open the door to this kind of crude utilitarianism. Rather it insists that there is an interconnection between values. This interconnection implies that if war is to be kept limited, then collateral damage must be weighed against the military advantage gained by the discrete tactic at issue, not solely against the goals of the war as a whole.[30] This requirement is not an a priori conclusion but one which has been derived from reflection on the experience of modern warfare.

This more nuanced view of the proportionalist approach leads to the same conclusion regarding collateral damage as does the interpretation of the traditional principle of double-effect outlined above. Collateral civilian casualties of a nuclear attack on military targets will themselves outweigh the military benefit in most cases in the European theater or in a superpower exchange. When this consideration is combined with the pressure toward escalation that civilian casualties will exert, then the conclusion should be clear. We should reach a negative moral judgment on any use of nuclear weapons which will cause significant damage to population centers. All nuclear attacks in Europe fall under this judgment. Both schools of thought on the direct/indirect distinction, it seems to me, are compelled to reach this conclusion, though they will reach it by different routes.[31]

All these considerations point toward a negative moral

judgment on any use of nuclear weapons by the superpowers against each other's homelands or by the NATO and Warsaw Pact alliances in the European theater. There remains one additional question to be considered before we can reach a clear conclusion about the scope of moral responsibility for the use of nuclear weapons. Much of what has been said here about the likely outcomes of any use of nuclear weapons by the United States and NATO depends on predictions of what the U.S.S.R. and Warsaw Pact are likely to do in response to such use. This creates two problems for moral evaluation. First, it is generally the case that we do not hold a person responsible for the actions of another unless there is a clear causal link between the act of the first person and that of the second.[32] Thus it might seem that we should not hold the United States and NATO responsible for escalatory decisions of the U.S.S.R., for such escalation would not, strictly speaking, be caused by Atlantic Alliance actions. The responsibility for the response and resulting escalation would lie with the U.S.S.R., not the United States and its allies.

On one level this argument is plausible, for escalation will not occur unless there is a free response from the other side.[33] However, to press the argument in a way which would absolve the nation which initiates the use of nuclear weapons of all responsibility for the actions of the adversary seems naive in the extreme. Such a stance is an essentially apolitical approach to the most important political problem of our day. The just war theory is a synthesis of moral and political wisdom. To argue the question of responsibility without taking into account the best political judgments of how an adversary will respond to one's actions is itself morally irresponsible. As Stanley Hoffmann has put it, "the criteria of moral politics are double: sound principles and effectiveness."[34] It is necessary to be clear that one is seeking only just aims by just means. But this is not enough. One must also be able to reach an admittedly prudential judgment that one's choices are likely to lead to the ends one wants to achieve through the use of means that one is prepared to justify. This is a political judgment, and it is not a whit less moral for being so. The arguments sketched in this chapter are based on more than a few such prudential political judgments. They can be challenged on the ground of political-military argument. But it will not do to say that we are not responsible for what the other side might do in response to our use of nuclear weapons.

The second question which this discussion poses is the most fundamental of all: the scope of our responsibility in response to the acts or potential acts of the U.S.S.R. There can be little doubt that the U.S.S.R. poses a truly serious political and military threat to the West. The military aspect of this threat is directed at the very physical survival of large numbers of the citizens of NATO countries. It is evident in the military forces, both nuclear and conventional, which the U.S.S.R. has deployed and in the Soviet leadership's stated willingness to employ these forces should this be necessary for their political purpose. Some would argue that the Atlantic Alliance would have no alternative but to make whatever military response is necessary to repel such Soviet aggression, including a nuclear response. It is certain that the prime responsibility and moral guilt would rest with any nation whose aggressive actions led to the outbreak of warfare. This responsibility becomes almost cosmic in scope if the conflict involves the use of nuclear weapons. Nevertheless, it will not do to say that moral responsibility for the harm which war causes lies solely with the aggressor. There are limits on what can be done even in defense of a just cause, and these limits are *both* moral *and* political.

The arguments presented here against the use of nuclear weapons do not represent a form of apolitical moralism that takes a stand for principle even though the heavens may fall. There may be issues on which moral and political judgment lead to different conclusions. But the question of whether one should use nuclear weapons in pursuit of a just cause is not one of them. The escalatory dangers which attend any use of nuclear weapons make their employment irrational from a political point of view, as well as unacceptable from the perspective of basic moral values and *prima facie* duties. The choice which we face is not between the alternatives of fidelity to moral principle and the effective political-military defense of Western society and culture. For the most reasonably predictable result of any use of nuclear force will be *both* a transgression of moral principle *and* a politically unacceptable outcome. In war between the two great nuclear adversaries of our time the logic of morality, of military strategy, and of international politics all lead to the same conclusion: the use of nuclear weapons can never be justified.

This conclusion follows from a judgment which is at once normative and prudential. Normatively, it rests on the just war theory's insistence that there are limits both to the legitimacy of the resort to force in the pursuit of justice and to the means which can be legitimately employed even in justified conflict. Prudentially, the conclusion arises from a judgment about the course of events which can be expected to follow on the use of nuclear weapons in a variety of different contexts. A prudential judgment, by definition, is not subject to logically certain demonstration. And in the case of nuclear war, the practical experience which is the ordinary source of prudence is fortunately unavailable. But the strong weight of the evidence from strategic studies is on the side of the argument advanced here.

Thus on the question of the use of nuclear weapons, the pacifist and the just war traditions converge. We can modify James Douglass's conclusion on the incompatibility of war and justice in the nuclear age as follows: nuclear war and justice can be seen to have reached an absolute conflict. Both the pursuit of justice and the commitment to peace demand the rejection of the use of nuclear weapons in all circumstances. I believe that this nuclear pacifist conclusion should be placed at the foundations of all future Christian initiatives for justice and peace.

This rejection of the use of nuclear weapons can become one of the building blocks of a new consensus within the Christian community on the morality of warfare. From pacifism and the original just war question this consensus will draw on the conviction that the use of force should be presumed to be unjust. With the pacifist tradition it has learned from historical-political experience that the use of force frequently leads to greater injustice and further violence rather than to the justice and peace which are sought. From the just war theory it draws the conviction that an assessment of the justification of the use of force must rest simultaneously on moral values and on political intelligence reflecting on the limits and possibilities of the pursuit of these moral values.[35] The achievement of the value of justice through the use of nuclear violence exceeds the limits of what is politically and militarily possible in the superpower conflict. For these reasons I conclude that nuclear pacifism—in the sense of the rejection of all use of nuclear weapons—is the morally demanded and politically prudent option in NATO-Warsaw Pact relations.

Chapter 6

Deterrence—The Hardest Question

The conclusion that the use of nuclear weapons can never be justified leaves unresolved the central question of how to prevent such use from occurring. In approaching this question we must enter into the paradoxical world of deterrence theory. Agreement on the unacceptability of any use of nuclear weapons can and does coexist with disagreement about the morality of the possession and threat to use nuclear weapons for purposes of deterrence. The moral legitimacy of strategic doctrines designed to deter an adversary from the use of military force through the threat to use nuclear weapons against that adversary has become the most controverted question in the nuclear debate today.

Indeed, the moral issues in the debate about deterrence must be faced even by those who do not share the conclusion that no use of nuclear weapons can ever be justified. Those who argue that some extremely limited use of nuclear force could be morally legitimate generally do so as part of a larger argument about deterrence. For example, proponents of policies which threaten and prepare to use tactical and intermediate range nuclear weapons in the defense of Europe argue that these policies are the most effective way to deter both nuclear and conventional aggression by the Warsaw Pact against NATO.[1] The same is true of those who support policies which project the limited use of strategic nuclear force by the superpowers against each other's homelands. They argue for such policies as the best means for preventing precisely such horrible events from occurring.[2] Pacifists too must face the paradoxes inherent in the moral debate about deterrence doctrines. Those committed to an ethic of nonviolence reject the just war criteria as an appropriate basis for the conclusion we have reached about the moral illegitimacy of the use of nuclear weapons. Nevertheless they hold to the conclusion itself even more tenaciously than do Christians who rely on the just war tradition. Thus they are faced with the challenge of advancing their own views of the best means for the prevention of nuclear war. Pacifists argue that there are forms of nonviolent action which can be effective in resisting unjust aggression. The pacifist branch of the Christian community, however, must ask the question of whether the forms of nonviolent resistance developed by Gandhi and Martin Luther King can in fact successfully deter the use of nuclear weapons by an adversary. Theologians such as Yoder and Zahn may argue that "effectiveness" and "statecraft" are at best secondary considerations in a Christian theological perspective. If their primary commitment is to the protection of all human life, however, they cannot consistently support actions which would make nuclear war more likely. They cannot logically refuse to enter into the debate about the best way to prevent such warfare from occurring. Pacifists may rightly conclude that the possession of nuclear weapons and threats to use them are immoral. But the rightness of such a conclusion will depend on the cogency of their argument about the best means of preventing war in the nuclear age.

Thus just war thinkers who reach the nuclear pacifist conclusion advocated here, those whose strategies include preparations for the possibility of limited nuclear war, and those who reason from a pacifist starting point must all face the paradoxes and ambiguities inherent in the doctrines of nuclear deterrence. These ambiguities arise from the logic of deterrence theory, according to which nations threaten and prepare for actions which we have concluded can never be justified. At the same time the intention which leads to such threats and preparations is the intention to prevent nuclear war. The paradox of deterrence is rooted in the fact that intention (nuclear war prevention) and action (the preparation and threat to unleash nuclear war) move in opposite directions. In order to achieve the goal of war prevention, deterrence policy threatens precisely what it seeks to avoid. It attempts to make the use of nuclear weapons irrational in the eyes of any potential adversary by making the consequences of such use unacceptable from any sane military or political point of view. Deterrence policy, in other words, uses irrationality as a tool of political reason.

The presence of this element of irrationality in the logic of deterrence is what makes these policies so resistant to intellectually satisfying moral analysis and evaluation. In a fully rational world, all war and all threat of war—especially nuclear war—would be eliminated. But this is precisely the problem which theories of deterrence attempt to grapple with: we do not live in a fully rational world where force and the threat of force have been abolished. As Richard McCormick has put it, "That is the very meaning of a 'sinful situation.' It is a situation we should not be in in the first place. There is no choice without some regrettable and destructive aspect."[3] In such a world it is simply not possible to come up with a clearly defined policy which does not contain something "regrettable" and at least potentially "destructive" within it. This becomes evident from an examination of recent attempts to formulate a moral perspective on deterrence policy. To clarify the issue it will be useful to look at several representative ways that moral theorists and religious advocates have dealt with the paradox of deterrence.

The moral ambiguity of deterrence strategy is reflected in the recent teachings of the Catholic Church on the issue. The Second Vatican Council took note of the fact that the theory of deterrence is advocated as a way of preventing nuclear war. On the basis of the theological and strategic thinking at its disposal seventeen years ago, the Council did not reach a firm conclusion on the moral legitimacy of the possession and threat to use nuclear weapons for purposes of deterrence. In the Council's words:

> This accumulation of arms, which increases every year, also serves, in a way heretofore unknown, as a deterrent to possible enemy attack. Many regard this state of affairs as the most effective way by which peace of a sort can be maintained at the present time. Whatever be the case with this method of deterrence, all people should be convinced that the arms race in which so many countries are engaged is not a safe way to preserve a steady peace.[4]

The careful and cautious formulation of the Council's discussion of deterrence is evident. The Council neither simply approved nor simply condemned deterrence. It noted somewhat vaguely that "many regard" this as a way of maintaining "peace of a sort." Moreover, the Council made no distinction between different sorts of deterrent strategies. Thus the Council's words throw little light on the contemporary moral debate between advocates of different sorts of deterrence postures.

Recent discussions of the issue within the Catholic community in the United States, as well as the broader political, philosophical and popular arguments, have not been as reticent as was the Council. But these more recent discussions have produced diverse and contradictory recommendations. These efforts to deal with the morality of deterrence show that the problem is an agonizing one for the Christian conscience.

The pacifist approach which is predominant among Catholics affiliated with groups such as Pax Christi moves in a straightforward way from a religious objection to all use of violence, to a condemnation of the use of nuclear weapons, to a rejection of a threat to use them, to a delegitimation of their possession and production.[5] As Archbishop Raymond Hunthausen stated this position:

> As followers of Christ, we need to take up our cross in the nuclear age. I believe that one obvious meaning of the cross is unilateral disarmament. Jesus' acceptance of the cross rather than the sword raised in his defense is the Gospel's

statement of unilateral disarmament. We are called to follow. Our security as people of faith lies not in demonic weapons which threaten all life on earth. Our security is in a loving, caring God. We must dismantle our weapons of terror and place our reliance on God.[6]

Archbishop Hunthausen's position in this passage is characteristic of pacifist appeals to the cross of Jesus Christ and to trust in God as the ultimate source of security. This is an essentially religious argument which subordinates the concern for the protection of justice through political means to the prime value of nonviolence. Nevertheless, Hunthausen supplements this religious argument with a military-political one. He maintains that the risks entailed by unilateral disarmament are less than the dangers we court by continuing to rely on nuclear weapons to insure our security. "To ask one's country to relinquish its security in arms is to encourage risk—a risk more reasonable than constant nuclear escalation, but a risk nevertheless."[7]

This second aspect of Hunthausen's argument rests on a comparative judgment of risks. As such it is a prudential military-political judgment. It points to the danger that the means which are used to insure the prevention of nuclear war (namely the stockpiling and threat to use nuclear weapons) can themselves increase the danger of such a war. But it is important to note that Hunthausen's stance does not eliminate the dangers of nuclear war, as he acknowledges in pointing to the risks which unilateral disarmament would involve. The unilateral disarmament position does not escape the paradox with which the existence of nuclear weapons confronts us. For both religious and military-political reasons he chooses to run the risks of unilateral disarmament rather than the risks of continued reliance on some form of deterrence. The theological aspect of this pacifist approach to deterrence cannot be made normative for a pluralist Church or a pluralist society, as was argued above. But the military-political assessment of the dangers of deterrence deserves careful consideration if the necessary limits to this pluralism are to be respected. This aspect of the pacifist stance presents a significant challenge to all theories of deterrence. Nevertheless, the pacifist option for unilateral disarmament does not extract us from the sinful situation in which large numbers of human beings face irrational threats to their lives and freedoms.

The National Conference of Catholic Bishops has addressed the question of deterrence a number of times in the recent past, and their statements help further clarify several of the moral issues. In 1968 the bishops adopted a position at variance with the subsequent statement of Archbishop Hunthausen. Though questioning all attempts at achieving security through nuclear superiority, they maintained that

> The Council did not call for unilateral disarmament; Christian morality is not lacking in realism. But it did call for reciprocal or collective disarmament "proceeding at an equal pace according to agreement and backed up by authentic and workable safeguards."[8]

Eight years later, in another pastoral letter, the bishops refined this position. Without adopting the pacifist unilateral disarmament position, they condemned both the use and the threat to use nuclear weapons against non-combatants. "As possessors of a vast nuclear arsenal, we must be aware that not only is it wrong to attack civilian populations, but it is also wrong to threaten to attack them as part of a strategy of deterrence."[9]

One of the most important episcopal statements on the question of deterrence was Cardinal John Krol's testimony before the Senate Foreign Relations Committee in support of SALT II on behalf of the United States Catholic Conference. Cardinal Krol repeated the earlier negative judgments on the use of nuclear weapons and on the threat to use them against non-combatants. He carried the argument a step further by distinguishing between threatening with these weapons and simply possessing them.[10] He used this distinction in an argument which has been repeated by a number of subsequent statements by individual bishops and which was incorporated into the first and second drafts of the pastoral letter presently being prepared by the NCCB Ad Hoc Committee on War and Peace.[11] He stated that the possession of nuclear weapons could be tolerated as the lesser of two evils provided that negotiations toward the reduction and elimination of nuclear weapons are proceeding in a meaningful way.

The Krol argument rests on three presuppositions. First, it assumes that it is possible to make a morally significant distinction between the possession of nuclear weapons and the threat to use them. Second, the conclusion that the possession of nuclear weapons is the lesser of two evils in the present situation presupposes a political-military judgment that unilateral nuclear disarmament by the United States could increase the possibility of Soviet aggression against the Atlantic Alliance. And third, it appears to imply that if arms control negotiations are not leading to meaningful reductions in force levels, then the Church would be compelled to challenge the moral legitimacy of deterrence as such.

The Krol testimony accepts the conclusion that any use of nuclear weapons is immoral. It sees the *threat* to use them as an indication of the presence of an *intention* to do so. It assumes, however, that the *possession* of these weapons is compatible with an intention *not* to employ them. But it also assumes that mere possession can serve as a deterrent, for unilateral disarmament is implicitly rejected on the grounds that it might well invite Soviet aggression. Thus possession must at least be *perceived* as a threat by potential adversaries.

It is evident that this argument is based on a complex blend of moral and political reasoning. Morally it presumes that both use of nuclear weapons and intention to use them are unacceptable. Politically it supposes that possession of nuclear weapons, without the explicitated threat to employ them, can in fact deter, for otherwise possession would be pointless. And finally it implies that these moral and political arguments can be combined without either logically or practically contradicting oneself.

The reasoning of the Krol testimony has been challenged from both flanks. The presupposition that one can distinguish between possession of nuclear weapons and the threat to use them has been rejected both by those who deny the moral legitimacy of nuclear deterrence and also by those who support deterrence but who contend that it cannot exist without a conditional intention to use the weapons.[12] The clearest argument by a representative of the opponents of deterrence comes from a non-pacifist, Germain Grisez. Grisez's case against the deterrent "is not that it involves death-dealing weapons, nor that they are nuclear, nor that they are used to deter."[13] Rather, Grisez's argument is against the intention to kill vast numbers of civilians through counter-city attacks should deterrence fail. Grisez argues that such an intention is an essential element of the present U.S. countervailing strategy. He quotes the United States Military Posture Statement for 1983 to support his argument that counter-city attacks are conditionally intended as a last resort by the United States. This is a murderous intention, and policies which embody it must be rejected on moral grounds. Grisez goes a step further, however, when he expresses his conviction that there can be no effective deterrent that renounces the immoral option of counter-city warfare. He concludes that we must abandon the effort to protect ourselves by any form of nuclear deterrence. Thus he reaches a unilateral nuclear disarmament conclusion on the basis of just war reasoning. As he wrote in an earlier essay, "When I say that the deterrent is morally evil, I do not mean that we ought to try to dismantle it if and when world amity is established. I mean that we ought to dismantle the deterrent immediately, regardless of consequences. The end simply does not justify the means."[14]

It should be noted that, despite the purist moral ring of this statement, Grisez's conclusion is at least as dependent on political-military judgment as it is on moral principle. Like all just war arguments it is a synthesis of the moral and the political. Grisez assumes (without argument) that there can be no deterrent without a conditional intention to use nuclear weapons against population centers. He further assumes, also without argument, that all deterrence postures are similar to the one outlined in the current United States Military Posture Statement. He suggests that the renunciation of the deterrent by the United States might lead to the loss of freedom in the West for a time but would ultimately show the inadequacy of Soviet ideology and lead to Soviet downfall. And finally Grisez asserts that reliance on deterrence simply compounds the evil with which the existence of U.S.S.R. nuclear forces confronts us. In his view, the unilateral renunciation of deterrence "is wise and realistic advice for salvaging the human good possible in our world. . . . The refusal to match others in evil is the only way for fallen mankind, individuals and societies alike, to stop compounding human misery and begin emerging into the light of decent human life and communion."[15]

These are astonishingly broad political judgments. Most of them can be questioned. Indeed I believe all of them, when taken together, present us with a false picture of what the political options really are. The reasons for this conclusion will be discussed below. Here it is sufficient to note two things about Grisez's just war argument for the renunciation of the deterrent. First, it rests on a synthesis of political and moral argument. And second, it does not advance a policy position which assures with any certainty the protection of the lives or freedoms of innocent human beings. Grisez's apparent moral purism does not free him from the dilemmas and paradoxes of the deterrence debate. Rather, it forces him to make some highly doubtful political judgments about the ultimate collapse of Soviet power and about the triumph of "decent human life and communion" which would eventually result from a U.S. unilateral nuclear disarmament. Pacifists such as Yoder are at least realistic enough to recognize that such hoped for outcomes can only be counted on in the kingdom of God which will be fully realized only beyond human history. But just war thinkers such as Grisez can be held to more this-worldly standards. From a just war perspective, therefore, Grisez's critique of Cardinal Krol's approach to the deterrence dilemma does not stand up.

The Krol testimony has also been criticized from the other end of the spectrum in the current debate. Where Grisez objects to Krol's willingness to tolerate the continued U.S. possession of nuclear weapons, Michael Novak challenges the

Cardinal's condemnation of the threat and intention to use them. Novak argues that there can be no effective deterrent which does not rest on a credible threat that the weapons in the deterrent force will be used. Further, there cannot really be a credible threat which is not based on an actual, though conditional, intention to employ them should deterrence fail to prevent the outbreak of nuclear hostilities. Writing in *Commentary*, Novak argued against Krol's willingness to tolerate the possession of nuclear weapons while rejecting the threat or intention to use them:

> The Cardinal was not yet ready to demand unilateral disarmament. Since weapons don't fire themselves, then mere possession, he conceded, is morally neutral. He did not allow, however, any *intention* to use them. This prohibition leads logically to having no deterrent at all, i.e., to unilateral nuclear disarmament. It also completely undercuts the moral basis of official US deterrence policy.[16]

It is worth noting that Novak and Grisez are in agreement on at least one fundamental issue: deterrence demands the presence of the willingness to use nuclear weapons. Neither Novak nor Grisez is able to imagine (or plan for) a deterrent strategy that is based on a firm commitment to avoid the use of these weapons. For Grisez, the willingness to move to counter-city attacks is integral to all deterrence postures. For Novak, any effective deterrent must be prepared for all possible uses of nuclear weapons. As he put it in a subsequent article: "A deterrent system must be reasoned and thorough; it must cover every major contingency. That is to say, it must be intentional; it must be the product of intelligence, foresight and will."[17]

This statement reveals the problematic aspect of Novak's argument. He is on solid ground when he objects to Cardinal Krol's clear distinction between the possession of nuclear weapons and the threat to use them. This distinction represents a kind of Cartesian view of the world which divides up reality into things (the weapons systems) and minds (from which threats originate). Such a clear distinction rests on bad epistemology and unrealistic sociology. However, Novak is on thin ice when he states that the deterrent must be constructed to "cover every contingency." This opens the door and even encourages a limitless arms race and an endless military build-up. Furthermore, Novak presents no criteria for distinguishing between the various types of deterrence policy and the force deployments which these policies call for. Unless Novak provides such criteria, his argument will legitimate *anything* a nation does provided it is called deterrence. Clearly this cannot be an adequate moral approach.

In order to develop such criteria for distinguishing legitimate deterrence policies from illegitimate ones, several points must be made. First, the relation between intention and action in deterrence strategy has several different levels which must be carefully distinguished. Were the intention that of using nuclear weapons and the action their actual use, there would be no question that both intention and action should be declared morally illegitimate. Deterrence policies, however, are formulated with the explicit purpose of preventing the outbreak of nuclear war. The actions implementing these intentions are not the actual use of nuclear weapons but military and political steps which attempt to prevent nuclear conflict. One must distinguish, therefore, between the intent to use nuclear weapons and the intent to deter their use. No simple logical argument can be made from the illegitimacy of use to the moral evaluation of the intentions involved in deterrence.

Nevertheless this does *not* mean that any and every strategic doctrine or weapons system proposed in the name of deterrence is morally acceptable. Quite the contrary. The factor that makes the intention behind a deterrence policy distinguishable from an intention to employ nuclear force is a reasoned judgment that the policy in question will actually prevent use. One must be able to make a solid judgment that the policy in question will decrease the likelihood of nuclear war if the policy is to be regarded as a true deterrent policy. To go ahead with the implementation of a policy which increases the likelihood of the use of these weapons is to *intend* this outcome. But to pursue policies which can be reasonably projected to make nuclear war less likely, even if these policies involve implicit or explicit threats, is to *intend* the avoidance of war. The moral judgment on the intention embodied in deterrence policies is therefore inseparable from an evaluation of the reasonably predictable outcomes of diverse policy choices.

In other words, it is impossible to reach a moral judgment about the morality of nuclear deterrence as a general concept. The real question for moral judgment is whether a concrete strategic option will actually make the world more secure from nuclear disaster or less so. There is no such thing as deterrence in the abstract. Rather, there are only specific defense postures involving diverse weapons systems, targeting doctrines, procurement programs and strategic master concepts. It is these that must be subjected to ethical scrutiny, not some abstract notion of deterrence or intention. Just as there is a wide diversity of ways that nuclear weapons might conceivably be used, so there is an equally large number of policies advanced in the name of deterrence. Both in the question of use and the question of deterrence, the moral conclusion will depend on a complex form of reasoning involving the concrete options from a simultaneously normative and prudential political point of view.

This fact is implicit in the Krol testimony, but I believe it is obscured by the way the questions of intention and threat are handled. It is also implicit in the Cardinal's statement that the moral legitimacy of a deterrence policy is contingent upon genuine progress in arms control and reduction. To make the legitimacy of deterrence contingent upon "meaningful and continuing reductions in nuclear stockpiles"[18] is another way of saying that a particular strategic policy must truly make nuclear war less likely if this policy is to be ethically legitimate. But the Krol argument moves back to the abstract level again when it concludes that, if the hope of arms reduction were to disappear, then "the moral attitude of the Catholic Church would almost certainly have to shift to one of uncompromising condemnation of both use *and* possession of such weapons."[19]

Rather than calling for a shift to a generalized condemnation of use and possession, a breakdown of arms control and reduction negotiations would rather be cause for moral objection to the specific policies which have caused such a breakdown. Such a response would more accurately reflect the fact that the real moral judgment concerns concrete policies, not abstract ideas about use and possession. It would also avoid the unfortunate outcome of removing the Church from the policy argument precisely at a time when its participation in this argument would be most urgently needed.

An additional issue in the deterrence debate raised by the Krol testimony which needs reconsideration is its discussion of the *toleration* of the possession of nuclear weapons as long as arms reduction negotiations are moving forward effectively. The intention of the testimony is to acknowledge that the risks entailed by the existence of nuclear weapons make their possession by the United States a genuine evil. This evil is judged tolerable if two conditions are simultaneously present: 1) the Soviet threat continues to exist, making unilateral nuclear disarmament even more dangerous than continued possession; 2) this risk is being decreased through effective arms reduction rather than increased through a continuing arms race.

The logic of this position is essentially correct, but it can be formulated in a way that will provide much clearer guidance in the effort to reach decisions about actual policy changes. The point of the argument would be more evident if the conditions under which specific deterrence policies are justified were more explicitly stated. These conditions are two.

First, *any new policy proposal must make nuclear war less likely than the policies presently in effect rather than more likely.*

Second, *any new policy proposal must increase the possibility of arms reduction rather than decrease this possibility.* This second principle is really a corollary of the first, for a sustained, open-ended arms race can only have disastrous consequences in the long run (and perhaps in the short run).

These two principles have the advantage of acknowledging that the moral judgment about deterrence is fundamentally a judgment about the direction in which we are moving. There is an intrinsic link between the direction of a particular deterrence policy and its legitimacy or illegitimacy. One cannot reach a moral judgment about such policies in a non-historical way. The possession of nuclear weapons is indeed an evil because of the inevitable risk of use which such possession carries with it. But the judgment of moral rightness or wrongness concerns the way human agents respond to the existence of this evil in their actual policy choices. The twin principles of reduction of the probability of nuclear war and increase in the possibility of arms reduction can provide more help in guiding such choices than can the general concept of toleration.[20]

The problem with the Krol testimony is that, although it recognizes the need to tie the legitimacy of deterrence to war prevention and arms reduction, it treats deterrence as a univocal concept. It does not distinguish between policies advanced in the name of deterrence which actually increase the probability of nuclear war and those which decrease this probability. Nor does it take note of the fact that some weapons systems deployed in a deterrent force will actually render arms reduction more difficult if not impossible to achieve. The same can be said of the position contained in the message of Pope John Paul II to the Second Special Session of the U.N. General Assembly on Disarmament. John Paul II stated that "In current conditions 'deterrence' based on balance, certainly not as an end in itself but as a step on the way to progressive disarmament, may still be morally acceptable."[21] This statement, though useful, is imprecise and not an adequate basis for distinguishing between different policies from a moral point of view. Like Grisez and Novak, both Cardinal Krol and Pope John Paul II seem to think that the issue is whether one should grant moral legitimacy to deterrence or reject deterrence altogether. In actuality the question for moral judgment is whether a concrete policy option will change the current situation in a way that decreases the probability of war and increases the possibility of arms reduction. To formulate the issue as Grisez, Novak, Cardinal Krol and Pope John Paul II have done is to treat deterrence in an abstract and non-historical way.

Several examples of how the two principles for morally legitimate deterrence would function in the current policy debate might help clarify the point being made here. On December 12, 1979, the Foreign Ministers of the countries party to the NATO military structure approved a plan which would call for the deployment of 572 new nuclear weapons in Western Europe: 108 Pershing II Medium Range Ballistic Missiles (MRBMs) and 464 Ground Launched Cruise Missiles (GLCMs). This decision was taken in response to the Soviet deployment of significant numbers of intermediate range missiles (SS-20s) and Backfire Bombers, both capable of delivering nuclear weapons on Western European targets. This decision was accompanied by a call to pursue the reduction of these Soviet theater nuclear forces, through negotiations, with the proposed Pershing IIs and GLCMs to be used as "bargaining chips." Thus, from one point of view, the NATO decision would appear to pass the test of the criteria of the Krol testimony and the Pope's U.N. message: the deployment of new NATO intermediate range nuclear forces was linked to a serious arms control proposal.

From the viewpoint of the two criteria for legitimate deterrence proposed here, this decision has a different appearance. NATO Pershing II missiles will have the capacity to strike Moscow within five or six minutes of launch. Their deployment may have the consequence of leading the Soviet Union to adopt a "launch on warning" policy for their own missiles. Such a step would seek to strengthen their deterrent against what is grimly referred to as "nuclear decapitation," that is, the destruction of the military and political authorities who are in command of Soviet forces together with much of the communication and control technology through which these forces are guided. Such a launch-on-warning policy would remove the awesome decision about the use of Soviet nuclear forces from human hands and place it in Soviet computers. The likelihood of accidental nuclear war in such a situation would consequently be increased by a significant degree. One must conclude that the deployment of these new weapons would make general nuclear war more likely, even though they are proposed in the name of deterrence. McGeorge Bundy has made this point somewhat more gently: "I . . . do not believe that it is stabilizing for one government to place the capital of its great nuclear rival under the threat of supersudden missile attack, and there appears to be some question of whether the American Pershing II may not have that capability."[22] I would make the point somewhat more forcefully: the new Pershing II Euro-strategic weapons fail the test for a morally legitimate deterrent according to the norms proposed here.

This conclusion is reinforced by the particular problems which the deployment of ground launched cruise missiles would create for future efforts to achieve arms reduction and disarmament. One of the keys to the achievement of mutual arms reductions by the superpowers is the mutual verifiability of such agreements. Because cruise missiles are small in size, easily concealed and highly mobile, the problems of the verification of arms control agreements will be significantly magnified by their deployment. Therefore, the GLCM component of the NATO decision of December 1979 is problematic from the viewpoint of the second of the two principles for legitimate deterrence.

It is important to note that these objections to the deployment of Pershing IIs and GLCMs in the European theater do not rest on a belief that Europe faces little threat from Soviet nuclear and conventional forces. This threat is indeed significant. The question, however, is not whether the Soviet threat is real, but whether the proposed new NATO deployment will make Europe a less unsafe place than it is now. If the arguments outlined above are correct, as I believe them to be, then the new NATO systems decrease European (and worldwide) security rather than enhance it. Thus it is in the self-interest of NATO not to deploy them. Such a judgment does not depend on an unrealistic attitude of "trusting the Russians."

A second example of the use of these two criteria is the

debate over the deployment of the MX intercontinental ballistic missile by the United States. The MX is a strategic missile with an accuracy and power sufficient to enable it to destroy Soviet ICBMs in their silos before they are launched. It is known, therefore, as a "first-strike capable" weapon. Its deployment by the United States has been urged for a variety of reasons, reasons which are not evidently compatible with each other. On the one hand it has been argued that the MX is necessary to close the so-called "window of vulnerability" through which Soviet ICBMs could effect a preemptive strike on U.S. Minuteman forces. This argument sees the MX as an instrument for strengthening deterrence. On the other hand, the MX has been proposed as a necessary component of the U.S. countervailing strategy which would deny victory to the U.S.S.R. in any nuclear conflict on any level of magnitude the U.S.S.R. might choose to conduct it. This argument sees the MX as a war-fighting weapon.

Secretary of Defense Caspar Weinberger has denied that the United States is "planning to wage a protracted nuclear war, or seeking to acquire a nuclear 'war-fighting' capability."[23] In the same statement which contains this denial the Secretary stated that the U.S.S.R. is designing and deploying weapons which indicate that "they think they could begin, and win, a nuclear war."[24] Weinberger then went on to argue that the United States "must take the steps necessary to match the Soviet Union's greatly improved nuclear capability."[25] Weinberger presses for these steps by the United States, which include the deployment of MX, in the name of deterrence. In his view, the United States must be capable of fighting a nuclear war and preventing the U.S.S.R. from "prevailing" in such a war if deterrence is to be effective.

There is something exceedingly odd about Weinberger's position. As Theodore Draper has pointed out, it calls for the adoption of strategic concepts and the deployment of new weapons systems which *we do not believe could be effective* if they were ever used. At the same time these strategies and weapons are precisely *designed for use,* not simply for deterrence.[26] For example, the MX missile is not simply designed to be invulnerable to Soviet preemptive attack (a goal which may be unachievable, as the debates about how MX should be based have shown). It is also designed to be able to preempt Soviet ICBMs in their silos. In the argot of nuclear strategy, the MX has "hard target kill capacity." Such first-strike capable weapons, especially when their own invulnerability is in question, invite preemption by the adversary. If an intense crisis were to lead one's adversary to think that these weapons might be used, there would be a strong temptation for the adversary to launch first in order to avoid having its own missiles destroyed on the ground. This, of course, would be an irrational act, given the likely outcome of any use of nuclear weapons. But the deployment of first-strike capable weapons embeds irrationality more deeply in the military/political structures of our world. Weapons such as MX transform deterrence into provocation. Thus they make nuclear war more likely and violate the fundamental principle of legitimate deterrence espoused here.

In the Weinberger position we once again come face to face with the way deterrence theory uses irrationality as a tool of political reason. But the Secretary's argument shows one of the great dangers of any threat to unleash the forces of chaos. This is the danger that the irrational actions which are threatened, and the steps which are taken to render such threats credible, will overwhelm or subvert any rational political purpose and transform policy into a vehicle of simple madness. Such would be the outcome of a deterrence policy that loses sight of its only rational purpose: the prevention of nuclear war. Policies which involve the deployment of first-strike capable weapons such as MX and which include war-fighting strategies seriously threaten such a subversion of political reason. Consequently they lack moral legitimacy no matter how many times the word "deterrence" is chanted over them.

It is policies such as these that have led many Christians to question the legitimacy of deterrence altogether. Both Hunthausen and Grisez represent a growing body of Christians who, from both pacifist and just war perspectives alike, believe that the time has come to oppose the very notion of deterrence. I believe, however, that as attractive as this position might be to anyone who takes the deep Christian aversion to all violence seriously, it cannot provide an adequate basis for response to the current policy debate. The unilateralist approach has a consistency to it that strikes a deep chord in anyone committed to the demands of both Christian faith and human reason. Nevertheless, this demand that anything that smells of the irrationality of nuclear war be eliminated from strategic thinking can lead to the pursuit of strategies which are both militarily dangerous and politically unachievable. Unilateral nuclear disarmament would in fact make war, including nuclear war, more likely.

To sum up, an adequate approach to the ethics of deterrence must avoid two antithetical forms of one-dimensional thinking. The first, represented by Weinberger and the current architects of U.S. policy, is a quasi-Machiavellian or Clausewitzian military rationality which loses contact with the only moral purpose of nuclear policy: the prevention of nuclear war. The second, represented by Hunthausen (for legitimate pacifist reasons) and Grisez (because of his failure to take the role of political reason in the just war theory seriously), is a quasi-scholastic or Kantian rationality that tries to deduce policy from moral first principles. Both of these "purist" positions can be supported by a certain logic and reasoned argument. The problem with each of them is that it fails to grapple with the complex relationship between morality and the dynamics of the international political-military plight of a nuclear-armed world.

The only adequate moral-political perspective on the complexities of the deterrence debate is one which recognizes that fully consistent, one dimensional solutions to the dilemma are not only wrong but impossible. The task is not that of eliminating unreason from our world, but of containing it, keeping it from getting the upper hand, and reducing it. As Stanley Hoffmann has remarked in another context, "What we need is the right kind of inconsistency."[27] The right kind of inconsistency in dealing with the paradoxes of deterrence will be a policy which has the maximum probability of achieving the goal of nuclear war prevention and the minimum probability of subverting this goal through the steps that are taken to achieve it. The moral-political debate about deterrence is an argument over where these two probability curves intersect.[28] Pacifists, nuclear pacifists and even those who believe that some form of "limited" nuclear war is possible have an equal stake in locating this point (or set of points) of intersection.

The two principles of reduction of the probability of nuclear war and the promotion of the possibility of arms reduction and disarmament state the norms which can shape policy with "the right kind of inconsistency." In my view the current direction of United States policy is shaped by the "wrong kind of consistency," a consistency that says that since the Soviets may have a "war-fighting" strategy the world will be safer if the United States does too. Once again, objection to this policy direction is in no way based on a sanguine reading of Soviet military capacity or political purpose. Rather, it follows from an analysis of what can be expected to result from the current direction of United States policy, namely a world in which nuclear war is more of a possibility and in which the hopes for arms reduction and disarmament are diminishing.

The moral issue in the debate about deterrence strategy can be stated simply: are the policies being advocated really deterrents or not? If they increase the probability of nuclear war or if they make arms control and reduction more difficult to achieve, they are not. Pacifists, nuclear pacifists, and even those who envision some forms of strictly limited use of nuclear weapons should be able to reach consensus on these two principles for the evaluation of deterrence policies. The great danger in the present moment is that moral judgments about the use of nuclear weapons will be adjusted to fit the logic of a favored deterrence posture. This appears to be happening in scenarios for limited intercontinental nuclear war, in preparations for tactical nuclear war in Europe, in strategic master concepts which call for preparations for fighting in protracted nuclear conflict, and in the rationales which are being proposed for a variety of new weapons systems, including Pershing II, cruise missiles, the MX, stealth bombers, and a variety of "third generation" weapons designed for the conduct of nuclear war from satellites and orbital space stations.

Such developments turn the structure of reasoning which is the only possible basis for legitimate deterrence on its head. They start from a consideration of technological and strategic possibilities. If, in Novak's words, a deterrent system "must cover every major contingency," then innovations in technological capacity and strategic thinking will lead policy around by the nose. It is an ugly picture: the human person whose highest vocation in this world is the protection of the common good through political intelligence is in danger of consigning this intelligence to the currents of irrational purposes and deadly imaginings. The urgent task of the Christian community, in collaboration and dialogue with all who believe in life and reason, is to keep this subversion of moral and political intelligence from gaining popular acceptance.

In light of this conclusion on the morality of deterrence, one hard question remains. If one insists that no use of nuclear weapons can ever be justified, is any credible deterrent really possible at all? Does not the condemnation of use render all deterrent strategies incredible or deceptive or both? In approaching these questions, the chief thing to be avoided is abstract and unhistorical thinking. It would be easy to conclude that deterrence and the rejection of use are incompatible were it not for a single, massive historical fact: large numbers of nuclear weapons are already deployed and ready for use by both superpowers. Though incompatible on the level of ideas and logic, deterrence and non-use are concretely and existentially interlocked in our present world.

This concrete interdependence of two realities which logically conflict with each other is a prime example of what it means to live in a world which is not fully rational and which is broken by sinfulness. In such a world the will to war prevention and the will to deterrence are necessarily linked. But it is crucial that we distinguish the will to deter from the will to use nuclear weapons. It is precisely this distinction that prevents the evolution of deterrence strategies into "war-fighting" strategies. If we had the choice between deterrence and war

prevention on the one hand, and no deterrent and war prevention on the other, the choice would be clear. But history
has not given us this choice. The choice we do have is between
policies which seek to minimize nuclear threats and nuclear
armaments in ways compatible with war prevention and policies which prepare for actually fighting nuclear war and which
open the future to an endless arms race. The first of these
choices is our only moral option. It is a logically inconsistent
position. But its inconsistency is "the right kind of inconsistency."

The way out of this inconsistency is neither unilateral
disarmament nor an illusory quest for ways to "prevail" in
nuclear conflict. The way out is the way forward toward policies which reduce the risk of war and which make disarmament possible. As Leon Wieseltier has put it:

> The proper conclusion to be drawn from the shortcomings
> of deterrence is, rather, that deterrence is not enough. It
> must not be rejected. It must be completed. And it is
> completed by disarmament, in the form of arms control.
> Deterrence and disarmament are complementary con-
> cepts.[29]

What Wieseltier is suggesting is the same point emphasized by
the two norms for legitimate deterrence. The issue is not a yea
or nay vote on deterrence, but the question of where we are
going with our nuclear policy. Moral policy decisions are gov-
erned by the effort to pursue moral values in historically and
politically effective ways. The logic of practical reason is not
identical with the logic of theoretical reason. On this practical
level the commitment to non-use of nuclear forces and the
commitment both to a minimum deterrent force and to arms
reduction are linked together.

In this context the central contribution of the Christian
community to the debate on nuclear policy will be that of
keeping public opinion focused on the central values of war
prevention and arms reduction. The Church should call its
own members and the public at large to scrutinize concrete

policies in light of these values. Policies which move beyond
deterrence to plans for actually fighting nuclear war should be
strongly opposed, as should the deployment of first-strike capable weapons. And an arms buildup which actually weakens
security rather than strengthening it should be named for
what it is: a violation both of moral norms and of political
prudence. By helping its members and the larger public to see
this interconnection between morality and political wisdom,
the Church will render an indispensable service to humanity.
In doing so it will also be exercising the ministry to which it has
been called by Christ.

Conclusion

This overview of the nuclear debate has surveyed the significant moral positions on the matter which are present within the Church today. It has reached three conclusions: both pacifist and just war approaches to the morality of war must be represented within the Church if it is to adequately pursue its ministry of justice and peace; no use of nuclear weapons is justifiable in the circumstances of the present international political and military order; and concrete policies advanced in the name of deterrence must be individually evaluated from the viewpoint of their contribution to war prevention and disarmament.

The first conclusion is theological and ethical. The second and third are ethical and prudential. Because these last two conclusions rest in part on non-theological judgments about the likely outcomes of military and political activities, it is likely that there will be more disagreement with them than with the first conclusion. Indeed some argue that the Church should confine itself to the elaboration of theological and ethical norms and the encouragement of moral virtue among its members while refraining from "official" pronouncements on questions which involve such prudential, political-military judgment.[1]

As a general principle this point is well taken. The abuse of religion and religious authority which occurs when the dictates of a political ideology are confused with the purposes of God is all too evident, both historically and in our own day. It is important to recognize, however, that Christian principles of political ethics are not timeless, transcendental ideas that can be discerned apart from the active employment of political reason and political argument.[2] It is surely true to say that some norms of Christian morality are timeless and non-political. But these norms are all of the *prima facie* variety. The Ten Commandments list strictures which are applicable in every society and in every historical situation. When we try to discern what these commandments call for in concrete decision, however, prudential judgment is always involved.

If the critics of reliance on practical political judgment in the Church's response to the nuclear debate were to press their case consistently, a considerable revision of the received historical tradition of Christian ethics would be necessary. For example, it is clear that the just war theory resulted from a historical judgment about how the values of peace and justice could be best served in a world where these values conflict. Had the Christian community refused to make any corporate prudential judgments about the affairs of the political order, the just war theory could never have emerged. The same is true of many other principles of Christian morality. It is assumed today that the transcendent dignity of the human person as a creature in the image of God *demands* opposition to totalitarian governments which seek to suppress this transcendence. With all who are truly humanists, Christians presume that governments must be constitutionally limited if human dignity is to be protected. This has not always been assumed, to say the least. It has become integral to the Christian tradition because of our predecessors' courage and insight in the task of synthesizing Christian faith and political wisdom. The same can be said of the belated affirmation of the right to religious liberty by the Second Vatican Council. Though rooted in faith and faith's understanding of humanity, this affirmation was a political act. It only appeared not to be so for those who took the right for granted. Less than a hundred years ago, a similar synthetic judgment was reached in the Church in the economic sphere. Pope Leo XIII and the American theologian

John A. Ryan convinced the Church that all workers have a right to a wage that will allow them and their families to live a decent life.

These references to the past show one thing. The Church has not been hesitant to reach conclusions which involve both moral and political judgment. The issue in the nuclear debate is whether the political-military issues are clear enough to allow such a synthetic judgment to be made now. I think they are. In the past the Church has largely been in the position of catching up to an already existing consensus. This has probably been right and good, for the Church is an intrinsically conservative institution. But on the nuclear question the tables are turned. Those who would conserve must say no to the direction being taken by our policy makers. In the present moment the historical consensus about the limits to warfare does not need to be created but protected. The weapons we have, and the policies we are devising for their use have created a new reality. This qualitative difference in our political and military world calls for a qualitative development in Christian moral thought. It will, by definition, be a religious development. But by everything we know from history, it will also be the result of political judgment. I think the conclusion is clear: *no* to the use of nuclear weapons; and *no* to plans and schemes for their use. Negotiations and strategies must all be bent to this end. This is the moral-political challenge to Christians in our time.

Notes

Introduction

1. Two helpful summaries of the evolution of the nuclear debate in the West are Michael Mandelbaum, *The Nuclear Question: The United States and Nuclear Weapons, 1946–1976* (Cambridge: Cambridge University Press, 1979), and Alan Geyer, *The Idea of Disarmament! Rethinking the Unthinkable* (Elgin, Illinois: The Brethren Press, 1982), Chapter 1, "The Third Nuclear Age."

2. See Christoph Bertram, "The Implications of Theater Nuclear Weapons in Europe," *Foreign Affairs* 60, no. 2 (Winter 1981/82), pp. 305–26; and Michael Howard, "Reassurance and Deterrence: Western Defense in the 1980s," *Foreign Affairs* 61, no. 2 (Winter, 1982/83), pp. 309–24.

3. See McGeorge Bundy, George F. Kennan, Robert S. McNamara, and Gerard Smith, "Nuclear Weapons and the Atlantic Alliance," *Foreign Affairs* 60, no. 4 (Spring, 1982), pp. 753–68; Karl Kaiser, Georg Leber, Alois Mertes, Franz-Josef Schultze, "Nuclear Weapons and the Preservation of Peace: A Response to an American Proposal for Renouncing the First Use of Nuclear Weapons," *Foreign Affairs* 60, no. 5 (Summer, 1982), pp. 1157–70.

4. See Stanley Hoffmann, "NATO and Nuclear Weapons: Reasons and Unreason," *Foreign Affairs* 60, no. 2 (Winter, 1981/82), pp. 327–46.

Chapter 1

1. See James Finn, "Pacifism and Justifiable War," in Thomas A. Shannon, ed., *War or Peace? The Search for New Answers* (Maryknoll,

NY: Orbis, 1980), p. 7; and J. Bryan Hehir, "The Just-War Ethic and Catholic Theology: Dynamics of Change and Continuity," in ibid, p. 17.

2. Pius XII, "Christmas Message, 1956," in Vincent A. Yzermans, ed., *The Major Addresses of Pope Pius XII*, vol. II (St. Paul: North Central Publishing Co., 1961), p. 225. For a careful analysis of this papal message see John Courtney Murray, *Morality and Modern War* (New York: Council on Religion and International Affairs, 1959).

3. Hehir, "The Just-War Ethic," pp. 19–20.

4. See, for example, Roland H. Bainton, *Christian Attitudes Toward War and Peace: A Historical Survey and Critical Re-evaluation* (New York: Abingdon, 1960), pp. 67–68; and Edward A. Ryan, "The Rejection of Military Service by the Early Christians," *Theological Studies* 13 (1952), p. 9.

5. For an excellent survey of the literature on this topic see Knut Willem Ruyter, "Pacifism and Military Service in the Early Church," *Cross Currents* 32 (1982), pp. 54–70.

6. Ibid., p. 55.

7. Bainton, *Christian Attitudes*, pp. 63 and 89.

8. For a classic analysis of this cause of the widespread growth of monasticism, see Ernst Troeltsch, *The Social Teaching of the Christian Churches*, vol. 1, trans. Olive Wyon (New York: Harper Torchbooks, 1960), esp. pp. 161–64.

9. Bainton, *Christian Attitudes*, p. 89.

10. See Hans von Campenhausen, "Christians and Military Service in the Early Church," in *Tradition and Life in the Church*, trans. A. V. Littledale (Philadelphia: Fortress, 1968), pp. 160–70.

11. James W. Douglass, *The Non-violent Cross: A Theology of Revolution and Peace* (New York: Macmillan, 1968), pp. 177–78.

12. Thomas Aquinas, *Summa Theologiae*, II^{a}II^{ae}, Question 40, Article 2. The translation is that of the Fathers of the English Dominican Province (New York: Benziger Brothers, 1947), vol. 2, p. 1361.

13. See Frederick H. Russell, *The Just War in the Middle Ages* (New York: Cambridge University Press, 1975), p. 296.

14. Peter Berger, Brigitte Berger and Hansfried Kellner, *The Homeless Mind: Modernization and Consciousness* (New York: Vintage, 1974), p. 89.

15. See Vatican Council II, *Lumen Gentium* (Dogmatic Constitution on the Church), Chapter V, "The Call of the Whole Church to Holiness."

16. For an important analysis of the relevant passages on love of

enemy, see Luise Schottroff, "Non-Violence and the Love of One's Enemies," in Luise Schottroff *et al., Essays on the Love Commandment,* trans. Reginald H. and Ilse Fuller (Philadelphia: Fortress Press, 1978), pp. 7–39. A lively discussion of the New Testament perspective on war and peace has recently been underway in Germany. See J. Beutler, "Friedenssehnsucht—Friedensengagement nach dem Neuen Testament," *Stimmen der Zeit* 107 (1982), pp. 291–306; J. Blank, "Gewaltlosigkeit—Krieg—Militärdienst im Urteil des Neuen Testaments," *Orientierung* 46 (1982), pp. 157–63; E. Brandenburger, "Perspektiven des Friedens im Neuen Testament," *Bibel und Kirche* 37 (1982), pp. 50–60; I. Broer, "Die Christen und der Friede," *Diakonia* 12 (1981), pp. 365–76; idem, "Plädierte Jesus für Bewaltlosigkeit? Eine historische Frage und ihre Bedeutung für die Gegenwart," *Bibel und Kirche* 37 (1982), pp. 61–69; J. Kremer, "Der Frieden—eine Gabe Gottes. Bibeltheologische Erwägungen," *Stimmen der Zeit* 107 (1982), pp. 161–73; V. Luz, *et al., Eschatologie und Friedenshandeln* (Stuttgart: Katholisches Bibelwerk, 1981).

17. Oscar Cullmann in *Jesus and the Revolutionaries* (New York: Harper, 1970) and Hans Küng in *On Being a Christian,* trans. Edward Quinn (Garden City, NY: Doubleday, 1976), pp. 177–213, both see Jesus as explicitly rejecting the revolutionary ideology of the so-called Zealot party. The writings of Morton Smith and Richard Horsley suggest that this interpretation is historically inaccurate, for they conclude that the Zealots did not exist as an organized political force during the life of Jesus. See Smith, "Zealots and Sicarii: Their Origins and Relation," *Harvard Theological Review* 64 (1971), pp. 1–19; and Horsley, "The Sicarii: Ancient Jewish 'Terrorists'," *Journal of Religion* 59 (1979), pp. 435–58. Despite this necessary correction in historical chronology, it remains clear that Jesus did not advocate violent revolution against injustice.

18. John Howard Yoder, "Exodus 20:13—'Thou shalt not kill'," *Interpretation* 34 (1980), pp. 397–98.

19. Stanley Hauerwas, "Work as Co-Creation," paper delivered at a symposium on the encyclical *Laborem Exercens,* University of Notre Dame, May 3–5, 1982. Hauerwas is here restating John Howard Yoder's interpretation of the ethical significance of the crucifixion. See Yoder, *The Politics of Jesus* (Grand Rapids, MI: Eerdmans, 1972). James Douglass has also written eloquently on the relation between the death of Christ and an ethic of nonviolence: "The logic of nonviolence is the logic of crucifixion and leads the man of non-violence into the heart of the suffering Christ" (*The Non-violent Cross,* p. 71).

20. James T. Johnson, "On Keeping Faith: The Use of History for Religious Ethics," *Journal of Religious Ethics* 7/1 (1979), p. 112. See Johnson's excellent book-length works on the subject, *Ideology, Reason and the Limitation of War* (Princeton: Princeton University Press, 1975); and *Just War Tradition and the Restraint of War* (Princeton: Princeton University Press, 1981).

21. *Summa Theologiae*, IIaIIae, Question 40, Article 1.

22. Johnson, "On Keeping Faith," p. 113.

23. Gordon Zahn, *War, Conscience and Dissent* (New York: Hawthorn, 1967), p. 256.

Chapter 2

1. James Childress, "Just-War Criteria," in Shannon, *War or Peace?*, pp. 40–58.

2. For the classic discussion of *prima facie* obligations, see W. D. Ross, *The Right and the Good* (Oxford: Oxford University Press, 1930), Chapter II, "What Makes Right Acts Right," pp. 16–47.

3. Ibid., p. 18.

4. Thomas Aquinas, *Summa Theologiae* IIaIIae, q. 64, art. 2.

5. Germain G. Grisez, "Toward a Consistent Natural Law Ethics of Killing," *American Journal of Jurisprudence* 15 (1970), p. 6.

6. Ibid., p. 76.

7. Alan Donagan, *The Theory of Morality* (Chicago: University of Chicago Press, 1977), pp. 86–87.

8. John Finnis, *Natural Law and Natural Rights* (Oxford: Oxford University Press, 1980), p. 92.

9. Ibid.

10. Paul Ramsey, "Incommensurability and Indeterminacy in Moral Choice," in Richard McCormick and Paul Ramsey, eds., *Doing Evil to Achieve Good: Moral Choice in Conflict Situations* (Chicago: Loyola University Press, 1978), pp. 71–72.

11. Richard A. McCormick, "A Commentary on the Commentaries," in McCormick and Ramsey, *Doing Evil*, pp. 224, 225, 227.

12. Ibid., p. 229.

13. Pope John Paul II, "1982 World Day of Peace Message," nos. 9 and 12, *Origins* 11 (January 7, 1982), pp. 476, 478.

14. Pope Paul VI, *Populorum Progressio*, no. 31.

15. I have not been able to locate the source of this statement, which has become something close to the motto of recent American pacifist groups. It is cited without reference in John Howard Yoder,

Nevertheless: A Meditation on the Varieties and Shortcomings of Religious Pacifism (Scottdale, PA: Herald Press, 1971), p. 68.

16. Russell, *Just War in the Middle Ages,* p. 308.

17. Gordon Zahn, "Afterword," in Shannon, *War or Peace?,* p. 236.

Chapter 3

1. See "Peace in the OT," and "Peace in the NT," *Interpreter's Dictionary of the Bible,* vol. 3, pp. 704–706.

2. Edward Schillebeeckx, *Christ: The Experience of Jesus as Lord,* trans. John Bowden (New York: Crossroad, 1980), pp. 695–96.

3. Yoder, *The Politics of Jesus,* p. 240.

4. Gordon Zahn, "Afterword," in Shannon, *War or Peace?,* p. 241.

5. For useful discussions of the relation between Christian love as self-sacrifice, as mutuality and as equal regard, see Gene Outka, *Agape: An Ethical Analysis* (New Haven: Yale University Press, 1982), esp. chapters 1, 3 and 8.

6. Margaret A. Farley, "New Patterns of Relationship: Beginnings of a Moral Revolution," *Theological Studies* 36 (1975), p. 646.

7. Childress, "Just War Criteria," p. 40.

Chapter 4

1. For discussion of this criterion see Murray, *Morality and Modern War,* pp. 9–11; and William V. O'Brien, *The Conduct of Just and Limited War* (New York: Praeger, 1981), pp. 19–27.

2. O'Brien, *Just and Limited War,* p. 27.

3. For an illuminating discussion of the meaning of intention see Donagan, *The Theory of Morality,* pp. 122–27.

4. For helpful discussions of right intention, see O'Brien, *Just and Limited War,* pp. 33–35 and Childress, "Just War Criteria," pp. 48–49.

5. O'Brien, *Just and Limited War,* p. 38.

6. For careful discussions of this principle compare Paul Ramsey, *The Just War: Force and Political Responsibility* (New York: Scribner's, 1968), Chapter 6, and O'Brien, *Just and Limited War,* pp. 42–55. Ramsey argues that non-combatant immunity is an absolute principle while O'Brien holds that it can sometimes be subordinated to the demands of military necessity. I side with Ramsey in this argument, but for reasons which are methodologically closer to O'Bri-

en's basic approach. For O'Brien, the basic imperative of *jus in bello* is that war be kept limited. I fail to see how such limitation can be maintained in modern war without a stringent interpretation of non-combatant immunity.

7. Michael Walzer, *Just and Unjust Wars: A Moral Argument with Historical Illustrations* (New York: Basic Books, 1977), p. 32.

8. See Walzer, *Just and Unjust Wars,* pp. 255–62; O'Brien, *Just and Limited War,* pp. 39–40; and John C. Ford, "The Morality of Obliteration Bombing," *Theological Studies* 5 (1944), pp. 261–309.

9. Stanley Hoffmann, *Duties Beyond Borders: On the Limits and Possibilities of Ethical International Politics* (Syracuse: Syracuse University Press, 1981), p. 27.

10. John XXIII, *Pacem in Terris,* no. 127.

11. *Gaudium et Spes,* no. 80.

12. Ibid.

13. John Paul II, Homily at Coventry Cathedral, May 30, 1982, no. 2, *Origins* 12 (1982), p. 55.

14. Hehir, "The Just-War Ethic," pp. 19–22. Paul Ramsey has pointed out that the diversity of interpretations is in part the result of an erroneous translation of *Pacem in Terris,* no. 127. *The Just War: Force and Political Responsibility* (New York: Scribner's, 1968), pp. 192–98.

15. Douglass, *The Non-Violent Cross,* p. 176.

16. See ibid., chaps. 4, 5, and 6.

17. *Gaudium et Spes,* no. 79; John Paul II, "1982 World Day of Peace Message," no. 12. See Hehir, "The Just-War Ethic," pp. 22–23.

18. For a discussion of the ethical dilemmas involved in revolutionary insurgency against repressive regimes, see O'Brien, Chapter 8. Jon Gunnemann has admirably analyzed the ideological and theological aspects of these dilemmas in *The Moral Meaning of Revolution* (New Haven: Yale University Press, 1979). For pacifist critiques of "just revolution" see Dom Helder Camara, *Spiral of Violence,* trans. Della Couling (Denville, NJ: Dimension Books, 1971); and Francisco Claver, "Prophecy or Accommodation: The Dilemma of a Discerning Church," *America* 142 (1980), pp. 354–59.

Chapter 5

1. John Langan, S. J., "The American Hierarchy and Nuclear Weapons," *Theological Studies* 43 (1982), p. 449.

2. Ibid., p. 453.

3. Ibid., emphasis added. For a helpful enumeration of the diverse uses of nuclear weapons which are possible see O'Brien, *Just and Limited War,* p. 128.

4. Ibid., pp. 452–53.

5. Ibid., p. 454.

6. *Gaudium et Spes,* no. 80.

7. O'Brien, *Just and Limited War,* p. 45.

8. Ibid., p. 135.

9. O'Brien is certainly aware of the importance of the dangers of escalation. In his discussion of the different levels of nuclear war he states: "The great problem is that once more limited means are used it may be difficult to seal off the higher thresholds and to prevent escalation that is politically and militarily unjustified and contrary to the norms of just war." Ibid., p. 129. If this is "the great problem" I would be happier if he had given it considerably more attention than he has.

10. See Johnson, *Just War Tradition,* Chapter VII, and O'Brien, *Just and Limited War,* pp. 42–43.

11. For a contemporary argument along these lines see Richard A. McCormick, "Ambiguity in Moral Choice," in McCormick and Ramsey, *Doing Evil,* pp. 42–45.

12. This is Paul Ramsey's argument for the foundation of non-combatant immunity. See "Justice in War" in his *The Just War,* pp. 141–47. Though Ramsey's reading of the foundation of the principle is not good history, it does represent a well reasoned response to the realities of modern war in the light of the Christian understanding of love of neighbor.

13. See Colin S. Gray and Keith Payne, "Victory Is Possible," *Foreign Policy* 39 (Summer, 1980), pp. 14–27.

14. P.D. 59 is scrutinized from two different points of view by Robert A. Gessert, "P.D. 59: The Better Way," and J. Bryan Hehir, "P.D. 59: New Issue in an Old Argument," *Worldview* 23, no. 11 (November, 1980), pp. 7–12. For a discussion and critique of the ways that U.S. policy has developed since P.D. 59, see Theodore Draper, "Dear Mr. Weinberger: An Open Reply to an Open Letter," *New York Review of Books* XXIX, no. 17 (November 4, 1982), pp. 26ff.

15. Harold Brown, "Excerpts from Address on War Policy," *New York Times,* August 21, 1980, section A, p. 9.

16. See Desmond Ball, "Can Nuclear War Be Controlled?," *Adelphi Papers,* no. 169 (London: International Institute of Strategic Studies, 1981), esp. pp. 37–38.

17. See John D. Steinbrunner, "Nuclear Decapitation," *Foreign Policy* 45 (Winter, 1981–82), pp. 16–28.

18. Spurgeon M. Keeny, Jr., and Wolfgang Panofsky, "MAD versus NUTS: Can Doctrine or Weaponry Remedy the Mutual Hostage Relationship of the Superpowers?," *Foreign Affairs* 60, no. 2 (Winter 1981–82), p. 287. Keeny and Panofsky present their arguments for this conclusion in the body of this article.

19. See U.S. Department of Defense, *Annual Report, Fiscal Year 1981* (Washington, D.C.: U.S. Government Printing Office, 1980), esp. pp. 65–67.

20. A helpful collection of these statements from U.S. bishops and a variety of other Church sources, both Catholic and Protestant, is in Robert Heyer, ed., *Nuclear Disarmament: Key Statements of Popes, Bishops, Councils, and Churches* (New York: Paulist Press, 1982).

21. Bundy *et al.*, "Nuclear Weapons and the Atlantic Alliance," p. 756.

22. Ibid., p. 757.

23. See Kaiser *et al.*, "Nuclear Weapons and the Preservation of Peace"; and the letters published in a section entitled "Debate over No First Use," *Foreign Affairs* 60, no. 5 (Summer, 1982), pp. 1171–80.

24. Bundy *et al.*, "The Authors Reply," *Foreign Affairs,* ibid., p. 1180.

25. Langan, "The American Hierarchy and Nuclear Weapons," p. 455.

26. See, for example, Richard McCormick and Paul Ramsey, *Doing Evil;* John R. Connery, "Catholic Ethics: Has the Norm for Rule-Making Changed?," *Theological Studies* 42 (1981), pp. 232–50; and Germain Grisez and Russell Shaw, *Beyond the New Morality* (Notre Dame: University of Notre Dame Press, 1974). The best discussion of this debate is the lucid and careful analysis by Lisa Sowle Cahill, "Teleology, Utilitarianism and Christian Ethics," *Theological Studies* 42 (1981), pp. 601–29.

27. Langan, "The American Hierarchy and Nuclear Weapons," p. 455.

28. Walzer, *Just and Unjust Wars,* pp. 276–77.

29. For an example of this kind of argument, see John R. Connery, S. J., "The Morality of Nuclear Warpower," *America* 147 (1982), pp. 25–28.

30. See, again, O'Brien, *Just and Limited War,* pp. 38–42.

31. See Johnson, *Just War Tradition*, pp. 219–24, for a related reflection on the two methods.

32. I am grateful to John Langan for having pointed out this problem to me in personal correspondence. It is of some importance in the current discussion of these questions among the military. He points out that Donagan's *The Theory of Morality*, pp. 37–52, is an illuminating treatment of the philosophical issue.

33. For further discussion of the philosophical problem of how the *acts of an agent* and the *consequences of acts* which flow from another agent's choice are to be distinguished, see Grisez, "Toward a Consistent Natural Law Ethics of Killing," pp. 76–78; 87–89. Grisez is using this distinction for very different purposes than are those who would use it to justify use of nuclear weapons even where escalation is likely to occur as the result of an adversary's response. The fact that the distinction can be plausibly interpreted to imply such different approaches to policy suggests that something important is being left out of the moral argument, viz., the significance of political judgments for moral analysis.

34. Hoffmann, *Duties beyond Borders*, p. 29.

35. This phrase is taken from the subtitle of Stanley Hoffmann's *Duties beyond Borders*. The synthesis of moral and political reason which undergirds the just war theory is well expressed by Michael Walzer: "At every point, the judgments we make . . . are best accounted for if we regard life and liberty as something like absolute values and then try to understand the moral and political processes through which these values are challenged and defended." *Just and Unjust Wars*, p. xvi.

Chapter 6

1. See, for example, Edward N. Luttwak, "How to Think about Nuclear War," *Commentary* 74 (August, 1982), pp. 21–28.

2. The view of Colin Gray and Keith Payne is representative of this approach: "An adequate U.S. deterrent posture is one that denies the Soviet Union any plausible hope of success at any level of strategic conflict; offers a likely prospect of Soviet defeat; and offers a reasonable chance of limiting damage to the United States. . . . As long as the United States relies on nuclear threats to deter an increasingly powerful Soviet Union, it is inconceivable that the U.S. defense community can continue to divorce its thinking on deterrence from its planning

for the efficient conduct of war and defense of the country. Prudence in the latter should enhance the former" ("Victory Is Possible," pp. 26–27). See also U.S. Department of Defense, *Annual Report: Fiscal Year 1981*, pp. 65–67.

3. Richard A. McCormick, "Notes on Moral Theology: 1982," *Theological Studies* 44 (1983), forthcoming as this is written.

4. *Gaudium et Spes*, no. 81.

5. See Joseph Fahey, "Pax Christi," in Shannon, *War or Peace?*, p. 63: "Pax Christi USA seeks to foster both nuclear and general disarmament. It believes that the construction and possession of nuclear weapons represents a profound immorality in the contemporary world." See also Joan Chittester's response to the first draft of the Pastoral Letter on War and Peace of the National Conference of Catholic Bishops: "My hope is that in the final draft of this much needed pastoral, the bishops will complete the prophetic work they have begun. Let them say a clear no to nuclear war and the possession and manufacture of nuclear weapons as well" ("Stepping Tentatively between Prophetism and Nationalism," *Commonweal* CIX [August 13, 1982], p. 429).

6. Archbishop Raymond Hunthausen, "Address to the Pacific Northwest Synod of the Lutheran Church in America, July 12, 1981," in Heyer, *Nuclear Disarmament*, pp. 134–35.

7. Ibid., p. 135.

8. National Conference of Catholic Bishops, *Human Life in Our Day*, November 15, 1968 (Washington, DC: United States Catholic Conference, 1968) p. 34. The passage quoted is from *Gaudium et Spes*, no. 82.

9. National Conference of Catholic Bishops, *To Live in Christ Jesus: A Pastoral Reflection on the Moral Life* (Washington, DC: United States Catholic Conference, 1976), p. 34. See the analysis of the ambiguities present in this statement in Hehir, "The Just-War Ethic," pp. 28–29.

10. John Cardinal Krol, "Testimony before the Senate Foreign Relations Committee, September 6, 1979," in Heyer, ed., *Nuclear Disarmament*, p. 104.

11. The first draft of this pastoral letter has not been published. For the references to the Krol testimony in the second draft, see National Conference of Catholic Bishops Ad Hoc Committee on War and Peace, *The Challenge of Peace: God's Promise and Our Response* (Washington, DC: United States Catholic Conference, October 1982), pp. 53–55.

12. For examples of these two responses, see Joan Chittester, "Stepping Tentatively," p. 429; and Robert L. Spaeth, "Disarmament and the Catholic Bishops," *This World* 2 (Summer, 1982), pp. 5–17.

13. Germain Grisez, "If the Present United States Nuclear Deterrent Is Evil, Its Maintenance Pending Mutual Disarmament Cannot Be Justified," *Center Journal,* Winter, 1982, forthcoming.

14. Grisez, "Toward a Consistent Natural Law Ethics of Killing," p. 93.

15. Grisez, "If the Present United States Deterrent Is Evil," forthcoming.

16. Michael Novak, "Arms and the Church," *Commentary* 73 (March, 1982), p. 39.

17. Michael Novak, "Nuclear Morality," *America* (July 3, 1982), p. 7.

18. Krol, "Testimony," Section I.

19. Ibid.

20. There is an illuminating parallel between the way the concept of toleration has been used in the Krol testimony and the way it was used by pre-Conciliar theologians opposed to the Church's acceptance of the right of religious freedom. The chief problem with both of these uses of the notion of toleration is their separation of moral and historical judgment. What I am proposing here regarding deterrence policy is analogous to the revision which John Courtney Murray made in the religious freedom argument: the recognition that moral judgments cannot be made unhistorically.

21. *Message of His Holiness Pope John Paul II Delivered by His Eminence Agostino Cardinal Casaroli, Secretary of State, on the Occasion of the Second Special Session of the United Nations General Assembly Devoted to Disarmament,* New York, 11 June 1982, no. 8.

22. McGeorge Bundy, "Deterrence Doctrine: A Need for Diversity," *Christianity and Crisis* 41 (1982), p. 387.

23. Caspar Weinberger, Open letter to thirty U.S. and forty foreign publications, printed in *New York Review of Books* XXIX, no. 17 (November 4, 1982), p. 27.

24. Ibid.

25. Ibid.

26. Theodore Draper, "Dear Mr. Weinberger," pp. 26–31. See Draper, "How Not to Think about Nuclear War," *New York Review of Books* XXIX, no. 12 (July 15, 1982), pp. 35–43.

27. Hoffmann, *Duties Beyond Borders,* p. 126.

28. This way of putting the issue bears a certain analogy to what

is known as the "maximin rule for choice under uncertainty." This rule calls for rational agents to seek the "best worst case" when the outcome of choice is uncertain, i.e., to act in such a way that the worst predictable outcome of one's action will be as close to what is desirable as possible. Since an all-out nuclear war is clearly the worst case imaginable in international affairs, a policy which aims at the "best" worst case is one which has the lowest probability of producing such a war. See John Rawls, *A Theory of Justice* (Cambridge: Harvard University Press, 1971), pp. 152–57.

29. Leon Wieseltier, "The Great Nuclear Debate," *New Republic* 188 (1983), p. 35.

Conclusion

1. The most recent statement of this point of view is J. Brian Benestad, *The Pursuit of a Just Social Order: Policy Statements of the U.S. Catholic Bishops, 1966–1980* (Washington, D.C.: Ethics and Public Policy Center, 1982). Benestad criticizes the U.S. Catholic bishops for overreaching their competence on policy questions and neglecting the more important tasks of evangelization and education.

2. The single best argument in support of this statement is the recent analysis and reconstruction of the lifework of John Courtney Murray by J. Leon Hooper, "John Courtney Murray's Ethics of Discourse: The Public Search for Understanding, Moral Judgment, and Commitment" (Ph.D. dissertation, Joint Graduate Program, Andover Newton Theological School and Boston College, 1982).